MAXIMIZE YOUR
MEMORY

MAXIMIZE YOUR
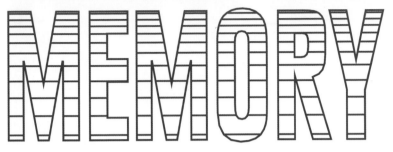
MEMORY

Techniques and exercises
for remembering
just about anything

JONATHAN HANCOCK

Reader's Digest

THE READER'S DIGEST ASSOCIATION, INC.
Pleasantville, New York/Montreal

A READER'S DIGEST BOOK

Conceived, designed, and produced by
Quarto Publishing plc
The Old Brewery
6 Blundell Street
London N7 9BH

Project Editor JUDITH SAMUELSON
Art Editor ELIZABETH HEALEY
Copy Editors GEOFF BARKER AND CLAIRE WAITE
Designer MALCOLM SMYTHE
Photographer ROSA RODRIGO
Illustrators SHEILAGH NOBLE, SUE SHARPLES, AND ROB SHONE
Indexer DAWN BUTCHER
Art Director MOIRA CLINCH
Publisher PIERS SPENCE

READER'S DIGEST PROJECT STAFF
Editorial Director WAYNE KALYN
Project Editor SUSAN CARLETON
Design Director BARBARA RIETSCHEL
Editorial Manager CHRISTINE R. GUIDO

READER'S DIGEST ILLUSTRATED REFERENCE BOOKS
Editor-in-Chief CHRISTOPHER CAVANAUGH
Art Director JOAN MAZZEO
Director, Trade Publishing CHRISTOPHER T. REGGIO

First published in 2000 by
The Reader's Digest Association, Inc.
Pleasantville, New York 10570 7000

Library of Congress Cataloging in Publication Data

Hancock, Jonathan.
    Maximize your memory: techniques and exercises
for remembering just about anything / Jonathan
Hancock.
        p. cm.
    Includes index.
    ISBN 0-7621-0242-X
    1. Memory 2. Mnemonics. 3. Recollection
(Psychology) I. Title

BF385 H275 2000

153.1'4—dc21   99-055958

IYM

Printed in China by Leefung-Asco Ltd

CONTENTS

AMAZING POSSIBILITIES

YOUR MEMORY IS PHENOMENAL. EVERY SECOND
OF EVERY DAY IT PERFORMS MIRACLES.

Every part of your life relies on memory. Whether you're walking, studying, relaxing, talking, playing—or simply breathing—some kind of memory process is always at work. Memory allows you to move, communicate, learn, compete, and stay alive. The billions of cells in your brain are continuously firing and connecting, accessing memories of words, faces, poems, recipes, stories, skills, dates, feelings; storing facts, jokes, movies, books, conversations, ideas; and filing and refiling, sorting and sifting, through immeasurable stores of information.

It's estimated that the average adult knows the meanings of up to 100,000 words in his or her native language, and retains information equivalent to an encyclopedia 10 billion pages long. It would take the world's most powerful computer 100 years to accomplish what your brain can do in one minute.

So why doesn't it feel like that? Why do you forget names, mislay belongings, overlook appointments? Why do you struggle with new skills, fail tests, forget jokes, lose your train of thought?

Do you feel that your mind is slowing down, embarrassing you, holding you back? This book will change all that. It will increase your confidence in your memory, so that you can put it to work in every area of your life. You'll learn how to harness the miraculous power of your mind, as well as how to apply it in the most practical ways.

The key to improving your memory is imagination. Memory relies on images and patterns, and you can learn to use your imagination to make anything memorable. If you doubt the power of your imagination, just consider what happens when you fall asleep and dream the night away.

TAKE A WALK
Right: Your memory lies at the heart of everything you do, even taking a stroll down the street.

DREAM STATES

When you dream, you can go anywhere, do anything, explore, experiment, take risks, and live out fantasies. Every night, you demonstrate the power of your mind to create vivid imagery and to write yourself into intricate stories.

The psychologist Carl Jung said that we dream all the time; we just can't see it happening when we're awake. He compared it to being unable to see stars in the daytime because the rest of the sky is too bright. To awaken the power of your memory, you need to discover how to switch on your imagination during the day. It's the answer to all your memory problems. With even a little imagination you can create exciting images and patterns that will help you commit anything you want to memory.

Would you like to learn and remember with ease, even in the most stressful situations? Do you want to abandon the habit of forgetting, and start making the most of your amazing mind? If the answer is yes, read on. You're about to learn all the skills you need to maximize your memory.

OVERFLOWING WITH INFORMATION
Right: Your brain is one of the most powerful tools for processing and storing information. Although you may feel it is already full to capacity and lacks a systematic filing system, you will soon learn how to increase its potential.

SOME MYTHS ABOUT MEMORY

I DON'T NEED A GOOD MEMORY
It's tempting to think that you can get by with the memory you have. It may be a little faulty, but you're comfortable with it. But should you be? If any of the following statements apply to you, there may be room for improvement:

"IT'S ON THE TIP OF MY TONGUE"
Above: Do you look at school photographs and recognize the faces, but can't quite remember the names? This is a common feeling that can be overcome with memory training.

- My memory used to be better.
- I often have trouble putting a name to a face.
- I often need to look up telephone numbers, birthdays, appointments, and addresses.
- I worry if I need to give a talk from memory.
- I find it a struggle to review for tests and to learn new skills.
- I can't count on my memory to work every time that I need it.

GENERAL KNOWLEDGE
Above: We all learn common facts at school, such as capital cities of the world, but these facts may be "lost" in adult life. Using memory techniques, you can make sure general knowledge stays in your mind for easy recall—in tests, quizzes, or even crosswords.

MEMORY WISH LIST

Now consider the areas of your life that could be improved with some memory training:

- I could feel confident about meeting and talking with new people.
- I could remember all the simple facts I need in daily life: telephone numbers, anniversaries, grocery lists, addresses, and recipes.
- I could talk from memory, and make my listeners enjoy and remember what I say.
- The essays, e-mails, and newsletters that I write would be memorable.
- I could become more organized, save time, and get more out of life.
- My favorite sports would improve, and I could learn new skills.
- I could be more creative, imaginative, and adventurous.
- I would be confident about my memory staying strong and healthy.

MY MIND ISN'T UP TO IT

"My memory," some people joke, "is what I forget with." If you find some truth in that exaggeration, you may be over-emphasizing the weaknesses in your recall skills and overlooking the awesome powers your memory has. When it works, it works brilliantly, taking you back decades, giving you access to countless names, facts, songs, and skills. In fact, you possess vast amounts of information from both your professional and private life.

Memory is about neither intelligence nor aging. The experience of remembering changes with age, but the latest research suggests that with a little training and practice, your mind can actually become sharper as you grow older. The trick is learning how to use your memory so that it works well every time you call upon it.

MEMORY TRAINING IS COMPLICATED, TIME-CONSUMING, AND BORING

People who fear confronting their memory problems frequently make these excuses. In fact, improving your memory should be relatively simple, quick, and interesting. When you use your memory inefficiently, mental tasks seem complex, long, and dull. In contrast, the memory techniques in this book will clarify and organize new information for you, transforming dull facts into vivid and memorable ideas. Learning will quickly become straightforward, quick, and fun.

MEMORY TRICKS

HOW WELL CAN YOU CONTROL YOUR MEMORY? TRY THE FOLLOWING TEST. WORK THROUGH IT AS SLOWLY AS YOU LIKE, AND SEE HOW CLOSE YOU COME TO THE RIGHT ANSWER.

You're a bus-driver, and at your first stop of the morning eight passengers get on the bus. At the second stop, three people get off and seven get on. At the next stop, only one person leaves the bus but a large group of schoolchildren climbs aboard: nineteen in all. Five people get off at the next stop, and two get on. At the stop after that, seven more people join the bus. At the sixth stop on the route, eleven people get off and four get on.

The question is:
What is the bus-driver's name?

Before you complain that you were tricked, look back at the opening words of the test. You know the answer—you just lost sight of it. You are the driver, so the correct answer is obviously your name.

It's easy to get sidetracked and to forget simple things that we've only just seen.

MISSING THE OBVIOUS
Below: When answering questions, such as the one used for the bus story, we can often miss the most obvious clues and think we don't know the answer. If you carefully consider the facts a couple of times over, you'll be surprised how much more you can answer than if you race through questions without thinking.

Here's another experiment. Read aloud this well-known phrase:

....

A
BIRD IN THE
THE HAND IS WORTH
TWO IN THE BUSH

....

Now look again. Did you read exactly what is written: "A bird in the the hand is worth two in the bush"? Sometimes we rely too much on our memory, and it can supply us with the wrong answer. In the bus-driver test, most people assume that they don't know the answer, when in fact they do. In this test, the opposite occurs: they assume too much and again their mind plays tricks on them.

But it's important to realize that we can also play tricks on memory.

As an example, try this memory challenge. You have 10 seconds to memorize this number:

6 0 2 4 7 4 2 8 2 9 3 0 3 1 5 2 3 6 5 3 6 6

Did you manage it? Perhaps there's an easier way to learn this information. Look more closely and you'll see that this is not a random list of digits. It's made up of some highly significant numbers, in a logical pattern.

60 minutes in an hour
24 hours in a day
7 days in a week
4 weeks in a month
28, 29, 30, or 31 days in a month
52 weeks in a year
365 or 366 days in a year

Now that you know how the number is constructed, see if you can write it down from memory.

Your memory power can be boosted—often very simply. Because of the way the mind works, tricks of the memory can be turned to your advantage without any effort at all.

TIME FACTORS

Above: Information, such as the number of seconds in a minute or hours in a day, is learned at an early age and is very rarely forgotten. This information can act as a trigger to help you memorize and remember more specialized facts.

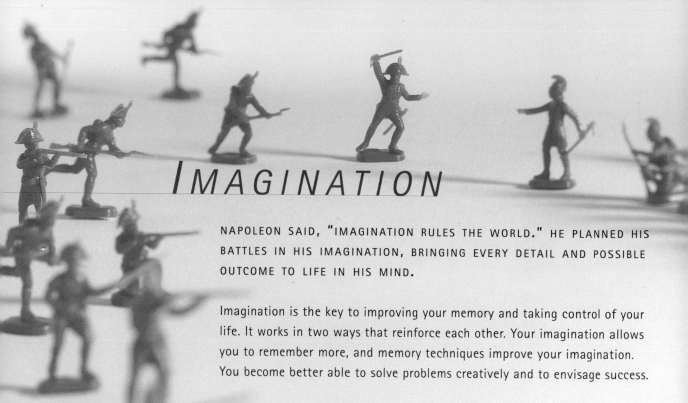

IMAGINATION

NAPOLEON SAID, "IMAGINATION RULES THE WORLD." HE PLANNED HIS BATTLES IN HIS IMAGINATION, BRINGING EVERY DETAIL AND POSSIBLE OUTCOME TO LIFE IN HIS MIND.

Imagination is the key to improving your memory and taking control of your life. It works in two ways that reinforce each other. Your imagination allows you to remember more, and memory techniques improve your imagination. You become better able to solve problems creatively and to envisage success.

Children are very good at using their imaginations. Remember what you were like as a child? You were inquisitive about things, testing them, exploring possibilities. You dreamed up invisible friends, played make-believe games, and learned about the world through imagination.

Children's books are full of pictures, and childhood stories are exciting. When we begin writing stories of our own, we're allowed to illustrate them in vivid colors. Unfortunately, though, at some point in school, we're told to stop drawing on our work; to use the same color for almost everything; to write neatly and use straight lines; and to work through things logically. The textbooks we study contain fewer and fewer pictures or stories. Imagination is pushed into the background.

To maximize your memory, you need to start thinking like a child again. It will feel a little odd at first, but that's only because you're out of practice. You can rediscover the way your mind worked when learning came naturally. Don't worry that your imagination might be too rusty. Here are some examples that prove it is still in fine working order.

SHARP AND TANGY

Picture a lemon. In your mind's eye, see its oval shape and bright yellow color, and imagine what it feels like to touch. Now see yourself taking a sharp knife and slicing the lemon in half, taking one of the open halves, and licking it. Are you salivating? Just the thought of licking a lemon creates a physical response—such is the power of the imagination.

Now picture an old-fashioned slate blackboard. Touch the surface to remind yourself what it feels like. Imagine that someone has taken a rusty iron nail and is slowly scratching it across the board. Does it set your teeth on edge? Again, your imagination was strong enough to fool your body.

Without imagination, you must struggle with material as it's presented to you. In this book you'll learn instead how to manipulate any kind of information until it is vividly memorable. Soon you will feel at home revisiting the childlike part of your mind. Imagination will give you control of your memory, and make learning effective and enjoyable again.

SOLDIERS OF WAR
Main Picture: Even at play, military strategists require imagination as well as experience and logic to execute their battles successfully and surprise their opponents. Developing your imagination is an invaluable tool for everyday challenges.

EXPAND YOUR SENSES
Above: The knife and lemon image is a potent reminder of how powerful our imagination can be in experiencing sensory memories.

GET MOTIVATED

This book contains information, tips, and exercises to help you succeed in every area of daily life. It's important to apply its techniques to as much of your life as possible. Whenever you learn a new memory skill, think of how you can use it in a real situation at the earliest opportunity.

The ultimate aim is to feel totally confident about your memory, so you'll be able to deal with any kind of learning task. By the end of this book you will feel that your mind is under *your* control, equipped with clear frameworks into which you can slot all the information you need. The techniques give impressive results—and they are no mere party tricks. Every one of them has a practical

benefit, helping to focus your thinking. Don't fret about clogging your brain: You'll learn simple techniques for clearing away data that you no longer need.

Don't be discouraged if some of the techniques seem complicated at first. Habits can be deeply ingrained, but you'll soon reap the benefits of each new approach. It pays to invest time in learning how to learn: Abraham Lincoln once said that if he had six hours to chop down a tree, he'd spend the first four hours sharpening the axe.

PREPARATION IS EVERYTHING
Main Picture: Abraham Lincoln stressed the role of preparation when he said "If I had six hours to chop down a tree, I would spend the first four hours sharpening the axe."

PRIORITIZE YOUR MEMORY REQUIREMENTS

Motivation is a key factor in any learning task. "What's in it for me?" we want to know. To help clarify your objectives, read the following checklist. Assess how important each skill is to your needs, and score it from 0 for unimportant through to 10 for crucial.

- Remembering lists: groceries to buy, jobs to do, items to pack.

- Learning names and being confident in a work or social setting.

- Remembering books, articles, and letters.

- Communicating from memory.

- Learning for tests and exams.

- Recalling directions.

  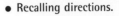

- Improving at sports.

- Learning foreign languages.

- Remembering recipes, skills, and procedures.

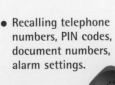

- Becoming more organized.

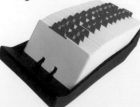

- Keeping your memory strong as you age.

- Creating a good image; speaking and writing memorably.

- Recalling telephone numbers, PIN codes, document numbers, alarm settings.

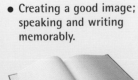

- Boosting creativity.

- Remembering birthdays and anniversaries.

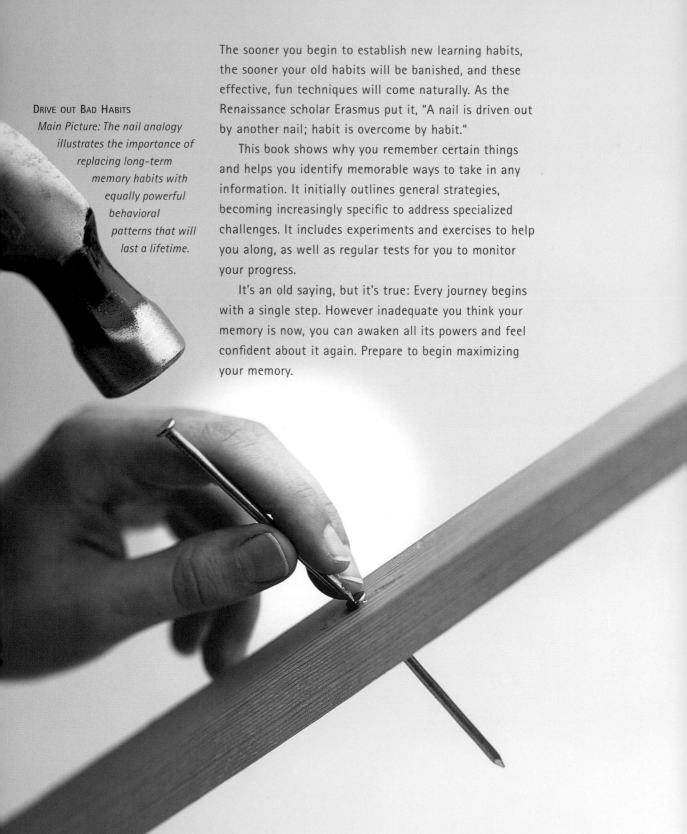

The sooner you begin to establish new learning habits, the sooner your old habits will be banished, and these effective, fun techniques will come naturally. As the Renaissance scholar Erasmus put it, "A nail is driven out by another nail; habit is overcome by habit."

This book shows why you remember certain things and helps you identify memorable ways to take in any information. It initially outlines general strategies, becoming increasingly specific to address specialized challenges. It includes experiments and exercises to help you along, as well as regular tests for you to monitor your progress.

It's an old saying, but it's true: Every journey begins with a single step. However inadequate you think your memory is now, you can awaken all its powers and feel confident about it again. Prepare to begin maximizing your memory.

PROGRESS TEST ONE

HOW GOOD IS YOUR MEMORY? BEFORE YOU START TO USE YOUR MEMORY EFFECTIVELY, IT'S INTERESTING TO SEE HOW GOOD IT IS NOW.

This test comprises four sections: names and faces; words; numbers; and lists. You'll need about 30 minutes to complete the entire test. Follow the instructions carefully, keeping strictly to the time limits. Don't worry if you're not doing well: Your success at the end of the book will be measured against your first attempts here. You'll find the test questions over the page.

WORD LISTS

MEMORIZE THESE TWO LISTS. YOU HAVE 5 MINUTES.

AGAIN, THE CHALLENGE LIES ON THE NEXT PAGE.

List A
1 strawberries
2 bread
3 matches
4 wine
5 turkey
6 cookies
7 cheese
8 baked beans
9 dishcloths
10 ham

List B
1 clean the car
2 pick up dry-cleaning
3 apply for new passport
4 take dog for a walk
5 return library books
6 meet Jack at the airport
7 write letter to bank
8 collect photographs
9 call Christine
10 book airplane tickets

NUMBERS

PRINTED BELOW ARE SIX FICTITIOUS TELEPHONE NUMBERS. YOU HAVE 15 MINUTES TO LEARN THEM. WHEN THE TIME IS UP, TURN THE PAGE TO TEST YOURSELF.

garage: 2562678
movie theater: 7890982
restaurant: 2550183

bookstore: 6277818
museum: 1290835
bank: 9389635

WORDS

GIVE YOURSELF TWO MINUTES TO READ THIS LIST OF 15 WORDS. TURN TO THE NEXT PAGE TO TEST HOW MUCH YOU REMEMBERED.

bottle
tree
horse
music
spoon
right
hole
time
fair
table
sail
break
heaven
drop
hand

NAMES AND FACES

YOU HAVE TWO MINUTES TO LOOK AT THE FOLLOWING 10 FACES AND NAMES. AS SOON AS THE TIME IS UP, GO TO THE NEXT PAGE TO TEST YOURSELF.

Angela Morgenstern

John Plummer

Pam Jackson

Janet Baker

Ricardo Montez

Luke Stevens

Maria Sylvester

Lee Chan

Nicki Fellini

Barry Benson

How Well Did You Do?

CAN YOU ANSWER THE FOLLOWING QUESTIONS FROM MEMORY?
JOT DOWN YOUR ANSWERS, AND CHECK YOUR SUCCESS BY
REFERRING TO THE PREVIOUS PAGE. REMEMBER, NO PEEKING!

WORD LISTS

FROM MEMORY, WRITE DOWN LISTS A AND B.

SCORE A POINT FOR EACH ITEM REMEMBERED IN THE
CORRECT POSITION IN THE LIST.

List A	List B
1	1 ....
2	2 ....
3	3 ....
4	4 ....
5	5 ....
6	6 ....
7	7 ....
8	8 ....
9	9 ....
10	10 ....

NUMBERS

WHAT IS THE TELEPHONE NUMBER FOR:

the bank?..

the museum? ....

the movie theater?...

the bookstore? ....

the restaurant?...

the garage?..

SCORE FIVE POINTS FOR EACH NUMBER YOU REMEMBER.

WORDS

CAN YOU REMEMBER
THE 15 WORDS, IN
THE RIGHT ORDER?
GIVE YOURSELF TWO
POINTS FOR EACH
WORD CORRECTLY
RECALLED.

....

....

....

....

....

....

....

....

....

....

....

....

....

....

....

NAMES AND FACES

WHO ARE THESE 10 PEOPLE?

GIVE YOURSELF A POINT FOR EACH FIRST
NAME, AND A POINT FOR EACH SURNAME
YOU GET RIGHT.

....
....

....
....

....
....

....
....

....
....

WHEN YOU'RE DONE, CALCULATE YOUR FINAL
SCORE OUT OF A POSSIBLE OF 100.
MAKE A NOTE OF THIS FIRST MEMORY
RATING—AND PREPARE TO SEE IT SOAR AS
YOUR MEMORY SKILLS DEVELOP.

RECAP

MEMORY HAS A BEARING ON EVERY ASPECT OF LIFE. THE BETTER YOUR MEMORY, THE MORE SUCCESS YOU'LL MEET IN SCHOOL, BUSINESS, SPORTS, SOCIAL LIFE, TRAVEL, AND EVERYDAY TASKS.

THE HUMAN BRAIN is the most advanced thinking machine in existence. Your memory has phenomenal capacity, and it works very well most of the time. However, it also lets you down, which can be a source of anxiety and frustration. The way to make memory work consistently is to awaken and use your powerful imagination.

Don't believe the memory myths. A good memory is vital to every part of your life, and you have all the mental capabilities you need to improve it. Don't be persuaded that age is a barrier to good memory; learn to keep your brain active and your memory will remain strong and healthy.

Memory techniques are not complicated. On the contrary, they help you to simplify and organize information. In fact, imagination is the key to successful organization. To tap into your imagination, learn to think like a child again: Be inquisitive about new information, and learn to explore it on new levels. Rather than struggling with information presented in a dry, straightforward format, learn to use your imagination to make any material memorable.

Finally, keep track of your motivation. Make sure you know why you need to remember and what you'll get out of it; and always keep in mind that the time you spend preparing is a valuable investment.

PATHWAYS OF THE MIND

IN THE POETIC WORDS OF THE ENGLISH

PHYSIOLOGIST CHARLES SHERRINGTON,

"THE HUMAN BRAIN IS AN ENCHANTED

LOOM WHOSE MILLIONS OF FLASHING

SHUTTLES WEAVE A DISSOLVING PATTERN,

ALWAYS A MEANINGFUL PATTERN,

THOUGH NEVER AN ABIDING ONE, A

SHIFTING HARMONY OF SUB-PATTERNS.

IT IS AS IF THE MILKY WAY ENTERED UPON

SOME COSMIC DANCE." THIS CHAPTER

EXPLAINS·HOW THE BRAIN'S UNIQUE

MECHANISMS WORK FROM DAY TO DAY.

WHAT IS MEMORY?

FOR AT LEAST 2000 YEARS PEOPLE HAVE SPECULATED ABOUT WHAT MEMORY MIGHT BE, WHERE IT MIGHT RESIDE, AND HOW IT MIGHT WORK, BUT TRUE SCIENTIFIC INVESTIGATION HAS ONLY BEEN POSSIBLE WITHIN THE PAST 100 YEARS.

INSIDE THE MIND
Above: Magnetic Resonance Imaging (MRI) generates detailed anatomic images of the brain. Primarily used for detecting diseases of the brain and spinal cord, it also provides an intriguing insight into our physical make-up and reveals the exact structure of the brain.

To Aristotle, in ancient Greece, memory resembled a wax tablet. Information was like marks inscribed in the wax. These marks remained clear for a while but faded over time. Despite his limited knowledge of the physical complexities of the brain, Aristotle appears to have understood why imagery and associations are important to memory. Plato, too, was fascinated by memory, and he recognized the value of memory training. Like Aristotle, he lived in an age when memory was worshiped as a goddess—Mnemosyne, mother of the Muses, who presided over the arts and sciences.

In the first century B.C., the great Roman orator Cicero wondered whether memory could really be "the traces of things registered in the mind." He had amazing powers of recall. He is thought, for

CHILDHOOD MEMORY
Above: Our physical memory develops most rapidly as children, as we learn to walk, talk, and think.

instance, to have used many of the techniques explained in this book to address the Senate for days on end, purely from memory. His questions about the nature and location of memory have been explored by thinkers and scientists ever since.

HOW DOES YOUR BRAIN WORK?

In some ways, the closer we get to mapping the brain, the less we understand it. What we do know is that billions of brain cells (neurons) interconnect and communicate, as pulses of electricity move across tiny gaps (synapses) between the cells. The chemicals that allow these pulses to pass are known as neurotransmitters. Deficits in certain neurotransmitters are associated with conditions such as Alzheimer's disease. Scientists are able to observe these communications in action and investigate what happens when strong memory links are forged. The clearest finding is the complexity of the internal communications. Connecting the billions of neurons, there are around 10 million billion junctions. Earlier generations attempted to pinpoint

the locations of particular memories, but it is now thought that rather than being "pigeonholed" in the brain, memories are dispersed among connective webs.

Some experts compare memory to a hologram. If you smash a hologram, each broken piece still contains the complete picture, only fainter. Others liken the mind to individual pixels—like the thousands of dots that make up a computer display. Analogies like these may give us some understanding of memory and indicate how much remains to be discovered about its mechanisms.

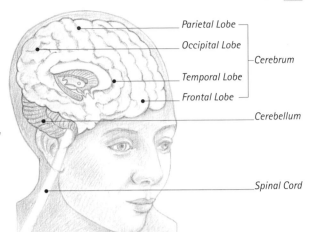

STRUCTURE OF THE BRAIN
Above: The brain, the control center for the body, is divided into two halves—the left and right cerebral hemispheres. The temporal lobes, located at the side of the brain, dominate memory functions and emotions, while the other lobes control motor behavior, sensory inputs, and vision.

IS MEMORY PIXILATED?
Right: Pixel dots convey nothing until they are activated with others. A word or image can appear on the screen, even move across it, as the pixels appear and disappear in various combinations—but can you say where the message is? Anywhere, nowhere, everywhere . . . ?

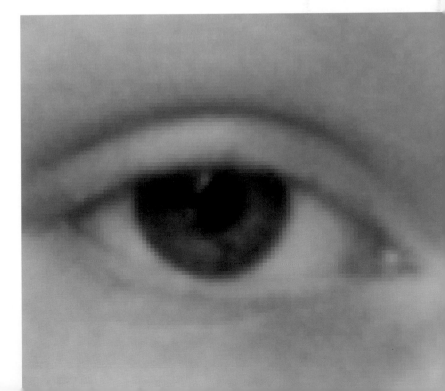

MANY MEMORIES

OUR UNDERSTANDING OF MEMORY IS FURTHER COMPLICATED BY THE DIFFERENT FORMS THAT MEMORY TAKES. TO MOST PEOPLE, MEMORY MEANS THE ABILITY TO REMEMBER EVENTS FROM THE PAST. BUT THIS IS ONLY ONE FUNCTION IN A RANGE OF MEMORY SYSTEMS.

Over 40 years ago, a medical patient known as H.M. was treated for epilepsy. The procedure involved drilling into his skull and removing part of his brain. He was cured of his epilepsy, but the operation had a peculiar effect on his memory. H.M. could no longer remember what happened to him, but he could still learn new skills—even though he had no idea where he had learned them. He didn't "lose his memory," because he had more than one kind of memory, as everyone does.

Imagine the following situation. You arranged to drive across town to meet Jack for a drink, and you're sitting chatting about old times when a woman approaches. Jack introduces her as his sister, and it turns out that she's interested in going to a women's soccer game for which you have tickets. She gives you her number, and you arrange to meet the following afternoon.

How many different kinds of memory were involved in this scene?

You remembered the date with Jack, and you recalled where and when to meet. You knew how to drive the car without much conscious thought, and you recognized Jack when he appeared. You were able to chat because you remembered thousands of words and could recall the things, people, and

USING ALL OF YOUR MEMORIES
Right: When we recall personal experiences, the presence of common items, such as a glass of beer, can be remembered precisely because they are familiar. Paradoxically, unusual events, such as a women's soccer game, may stick in our minds because they are out of the ordinary.

SING A SWEET SONG
Below: Musical melodies and rhythms are extremely memorable, as they reflect emotive, personal experiences.

ideas to which they referred. Your memories of the past came to life as you talked through old times. You took in new information when Jack's sister arrived, and you created a memory to meet her the next day.

Of course you also remembered how to drink at the same time as thinking back into the past and listening to Jack. And while driving you absorbed new details about your surroundings while singing along to a tune on the radio and remembering where you were when you first heard it . . .

This scene highlights the four main types of memory and the ways in which they overlap.

EPISODIC MEMORY

Episodic memory records events from the past. This kind of recall can easily play tricks on us. If you investigate your earliest memories, for example, it's likely that you'll discover a great many inaccuracies. Pick a moment when a particular world event happened, and think where you were when you heard about it. You've probably described this to others—but how true is your recollection? Consider all of the details—diary entries, photographs, and the memories of other people. Episodic memory lets you down more often than you might think.

It's your episodic memory that helps you remember youthful memories.

SEMANTIC MEMORY

Semantic memory holds knowledge of the world. You remember what a cat is, what your telephone number is, and that the earth revolves around the sun. Episodic and semantic memory are intertwined, but they seem to operate from different areas in the brain. That's why people can experience a failure of one without noticeable change in the other. A stroke victim, for example, may be able to remember where the sugar is kept (episodic), but be unable to recall the word for the sweet white granules (semantic).

General knowledge, mostly learned when young, is managed by your semantic memory.

COMPARING EPISODIC AND SEMANTIC MEMORIES

Compare your episodic and semantic memory with this test. You have exactly one minute to write down as many words as you can beginning with the letter S.

As soon as you're finished, give yourself another minute to write down as many items of food (not drink) as you can, beginning with any letters you like. Now compare the two lists. Are they roughly the same length, or is the first longer than the second?

This is a test traditionally used to diagnose semantic memory loss. Most people write about the same number of words in each list, but people who have problems with their semantic memory manage considerably fewer words on the second list. They can remember words connected simply by their appearance—the same initial letter—but find it much harder to recall words to fit into a meaningful group—in this case, foods. These are the four traditional categories of memory, but just as the mind

BEAT THE CLOCK
Right: A common way to test your memory is to give yourself a limited time period for recalling information. This is especially good fun with a friend.

PROCEDURAL MEMORY

Procedural memory takes care of those skills we "never forget." Every day we perform countless tasks that require no conscious thought—walking, swimming, dancing—and these memories are the most resilient of all. In many cases, people with serious memory loss retain an ability to play a musical instrument.

Procedural memory takes care of skills such as riding a bicycle.

PROSPECTIVE MEMORY

Prospective memory allows us to plan our future. Considering how many things we can forget, it's not surprising that this is one of the weakest types of memory. Sense triggers can remind us of the past, but are much less likely to prompt us about a future task.

Prospective memory can be harnessed to help us plan out the future.

works through complex interconnections, so their functions continually overlap. While practicing a new tai ch'i movement, for example, you could be using episodic memory (what was said at the end of the last class), semantic memory (what tai ch'i means), procedural memory (how to do tai ch'i), and finally prospective memory (the date on which the next practice session is scheduled).

The memory techniques outlined in this book can boost all four types of memory. Also, because they correspond to the mind's natural workings, these techniques can help anyone improve their memory. While scientists inch forward in their knowledge of brain functioning, you can discover how your memory works in practice.

The following pages describe a range of tests designed to highlight the kinds of information you remember best, and the areas where your memory is weakest. Understanding the natural strengths of your mind is a key step toward making it work successfully all the time.

OVERLAPPING MEMORIES
Left: Physical activities, such as tai ch'i or horseback riding, are perfect examples of how different types of memory are used in combination.

THE WAY YOUR MEMORY WORKS IN PRACTICE

THESE EXERCISES TEST YOUR FOUR TYPES OF MEMORY,
SO YOU CAN SEE HOW EACH TYPE OPERATES IN PRACTICE.

STORIES

ASK A FRIEND TO READ
STORY A TO YOU. WHEN
STORY A IS FINISHED,
WAIT A FEW MINUTES,
AND THEN HAVE YOUR
FRIEND READ OUT STORY
B IN THE SAME WAY.
YOU'LL BE ASKED
QUESTION ABOUT THE
STORIES LATER.

Story A

Jill was walking through the woods to her aunt's house. It was her aunt's birthday, and Jill had a present for her: a new china teapot. Jill had wrapped it as best she could, but the spout was sticking out of the paper, and she hoped her aunt wouldn't mind.

Suddenly, Jill came across a huge toadstool on the path, blocking her way. Inspecting the toadstool—which was taller than she was—she noticed that there was a window in the stem, but it was too dirty to see through. "Is there a door anywhere?," she wondered. She walked all around the toadstool, but couldn't see any way in.

Jill longed to have a look inside this strange toadstool, and she sat down under a nearby tree while she pondered what to do. She leaned her head against the tree trunk—and suddenly, with a loud creak, a hidden door in the stem of the toadstool sprang open. She must have discovered a secret mechanism. Jill slipped through the door.

Inside, the toadstool seemed even bigger than it had looked from outside. There was a staircase at Jill's feet leading into the ground, and she held onto the bright blue railing as she picked her way downward. Paintings of cats and dogs were on the walls, although it was difficult to see the details in the dim light. Suddenly, the stairs came to an end in front of a red door. Jill heard loud rock music, and she thought she could smell burning . . .

Story B

Jack was wandering along the beach looking for the friends who'd promised to meet him there. He was carrying his swim trunks in a bag, along with some sunscreen and a baseball cap. There was no sign of his friends, so he bought an ice cream, then built a sandcastle. After a while he lay down and went to sleep.

When Jack awoke, his friends were nowhere to be seen. He bought a drink and a book and sat reading, looking up every so often for his friends.

The beach was very crowded. Jack watched people swimming, playing ball, walking dogs, and flying kites—but where were his friends? He checked his diary: It was August 15; this was the right beach; and it was well after two o'clock, the time they'd agreed—so where were they?

Jack was hungry again, so he bought a hotdog and some fries. He walked along the water's edge, watching water-skiers and people in boats. A ball game had begun, and Jack stopped for a moment to watch.

Continuing his walk, he saw children building sandcastles and sunbathers enjoying the weather. By the time Jack reached the end of the beach he was ready to give up—when, from the distance, he heard familiar voices . . .

FACES

LOOK AT THESE THREE MEN. LATER YOU'LL NEED TO PICK ONE OF THEM FROM A POLICE LINE-UP.

PICTURES

PRINTED BELOW ARE 20 RANDOM IMAGES. SPEND A COUPLE OF SECONDS LOOKING AT EACH PICTURE. LATER YOU'LL BE ASKED HOW MANY OF THEM YOU CAN RECOGNIZE.

NUMBERS

4

3 6

7 4 9

0 3 7 1

9 4 1 6 4

5 5 9 8 1 0

7 8 3 4 1 8 9

4 0 9 1 2 8 5 2

9 4 7 7 8 3 1 0 9

7 6 8 3 7 5 9 8 2 2

9 8 2 3 9 4 0 9 7 1 3

8 1 3 9 7 7 3 6 4 8 2 7

ENLIST THE HELP OF YOUR FRIEND AGAIN TO READ ALOUD EACH OF THESE ROWS OF NUMBERS, DIGIT BY DIGIT, AT A REGULAR RATE. AFTER EACH LINE IS READ OUT, SEE HOW MANY OF THE NUMBERS YOU CAN REPEAT FROM MEMORY, STARTING WITH THE FIRST NUMBER EACH TIME. THE AIM IS TO DISCOVER HOW MANY DIGITS YOU CAN REMEMBER AT ONCE.

WORD LIST

HERE'S ANOTHER EXPERIMENT THAT WORKS BEST WITH SOME HELP FROM ANOTHER PERSON. ASK YOUR FRIEND TO READ YOU THE FOLLOWING LIST OF 25 WORDS. AS SOON AS YOU'VE HEARD THEM ALL, WRITE DOWN AS MANY OF THEM AS YOU CAN, IN ANY ORDER, FROM MEMORY.

Tyrannosaurus-Rex	key
blue	cedar
famine	ear
Elvis	coat
sense	scissors
elm	pencil
time	pine
box	dog
yesterday	light
hole	paper
wine	welcome
bar	oak

PUT YOUR ANSWER-PAPER ASIDE FOR NOW, BUT YOU'LL NEED IT LATER WHEN YOUR RESPONSES ARE ANALYZED.

PATTERNS

LOOK AT BOX A (BELOW LEFT) FOR ONE SECOND, THEN CLOSE YOUR EYES, SHUT THE BOOK AND DECIDE HOW MANY DOTS THERE ARE IN THE BOX. CHECK YOUR SUCCESS, THEN REPEAT THIS PROCEDURE FOR BOX B (BELOW RIGHT).

Box A

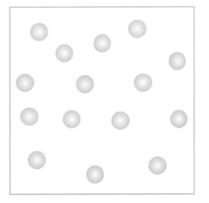

Box B

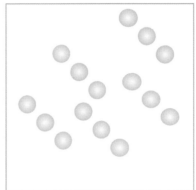

EIGHT QUESTIONS TO GET YOU THINKING

ANSWER THE FOLLOWING QUESTIONS DESIGNED TO HELP YOU EXPLORE THE WAY YOUR MEMORY WORKS:

1. What was the weather like two weeks ago today?

2. Pick any coin you use regularly. From memory, describe its design.

3. What is your home telephone number?

4. Describe an embarrassing moment in your life.

5. Is blemf a real word?

6. What was the weather like the last time you played a sport?

7. What was Leonardo da Vinci's telephone number?

8. In an apple, which way do the seeds point?

FACES: PART TWO

ON PAGE 29, YOU SAW PHOTOGRAPHS OF THREE MEN. WITHOUT LOOKING AT THEM AGAIN, SEE IF YOU CAN SPOT ONE OF THEM IN THE LINE-UP BELOW. YOU'RE LOOKING FOR THE MAN WHO WAS CARRYING A BRIEFCASE.

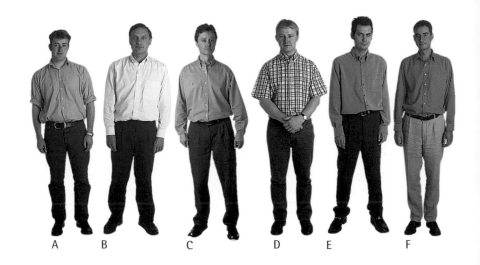

A   B   C   D   E   F

STORIES: PART TWO

ASK YOUR FRIEND TO TAKE THE BOOK AND TURN BACK TO PAGE 28. RETELL STORY A FROM MEMORY, INCLUDING AS MANY DETAILS AS YOU CAN ABOUT JILL'S ADVENTURE. THEN DO THE SAME FOR STORY B—JACK'S DAY AT THE BEACH. IT'S UP TO YOUR FRIEND TO DECIDE WHICH OF THE TWO STORIES YOU COULD REMEMBER WITH GREATER ACCURACY, AND TO POINT OUT ANY DETAILS YOU GOT WRONG, FORGOT, OR ADDED.

PICTURES: PART TWO

ON THE OPPOSITE PAGE ARE 40 IMAGES. YOU SAW 20 OF THEM BEFORE, BUT CAN YOU RECOGNIZE THEM NOW? JOT DOWN THE NUMBERS OF THE PICTURES YOU THINK APPEARED EARLIER, THEN TURN BACK TO PAGE 30 TO CHECK YOUR SUCCESS.

GETTING SWITCHED ON

WE ALL REMEMBER LARGE AMOUNTS OF INFORMATION, BUT WE ALSO FORGET A GREAT DEAL.

In the Eight Questions on page 31, how well did you describe the coin? As for the apple, its seeds point upward towards the stalk. This was one of the questions that researcher J. McKeen Cattell asked students in 1895 to highlight a fundamental rule about memory: Having seen something is no guarantee that you will remember it. Other questions asked by Cattell included: Are chestnut or oak trees the first to lose their leaves in autumn? Do horses stand with their heads or their tails to the wind? These were things that the students had seen many times—yet their replies were scarcely more accurate than their answers to random questions. Only 59 percent knew that chestnut trees lose their leaves first; 64 percent remembered that horses stand with their tails to the wind; and just 39 percent knew about the apple.

THE BIG APPLE
Main Picture: Unchanging characteristics of the natural world often go unnoticed. The apple-seed example highlights how easy it is to be exposed to such information on a regular basis without it registering in our memories.

"[People] cannot state much better what the weather was a week ago than what it will be a week hence!" Cattell remarked on finding that only seven from a group of 56 remembered the weather from one week earlier. Without a reason to remember, most people will forget. Important factors in activating your memory include:

INDELIBLE IMAGES
Below: The Haber experiment illustrates the power of visual images over the written and spoken word.

IMAGERY

How well did you score on the pictures exercise on page 30? Most people pick out most—if not all—of the original 20 images. In the 1970s, *Scientific American* magazine published the work of memory researcher Ralph Haber. He investigated people's ability to recognize pictures, and was amazed by the results. Each volunteer was shown 2,500 slides, seeing one image every 10 seconds. After an hour-long break, the volunteers were shown 2,500 pairs of slides. One image in each pair was from the original set, and the volunteers simply had to say which one they thought it was.

The accuracy rate was between 80 and 95 percent. Haber wrote that these experiments "suggest that recognition of pictures is essentially perfect. The results would probably have been the same if we had used 25,000 pictures."

The memory loves pictures. When you hear a voice on the telephone, it's natural to imagine what the speaker looks like. Poetry uses vivid imagery, and brand images are easily imprinted on the consumer's mind. In the word list on page 31, you're more likely to have recalled words that you could picture (Elvis, dog) than the abstract words, such as chance. Because the mind relishes imagery, memory techniques usually involve creating memorable pictures.

How about the faces exercise? Did you pick the correct man from the line-up (photograph C)? This was difficult because you didn't know which man to remember, and the man you wanted looked different when he appeared again. This highlights that your memory always needs to be controlled carefully.

ODDITIES

In the word list, Tyrannosaurus Rex is much more memorable than everyday words such as coat. We tend to remember our unusual experiences, just as we remember strange stories more readily than the mundane ones. You're more likely to have recalled the surreal details of Story A on page 28, than the dull recital of Story B on page 29.

CONNECTIONS

There are other reasons why Jill's story is more memorable. Story A is a series of connected events and there's a reason for everything. Jill is walking through the woods because she's on her way to visit her aunt for her birthday. She stops because there's something blocking her path, and so on. Story B is a loose collection of events— buying a hotdog, going to sleep—and could have happened in any order.

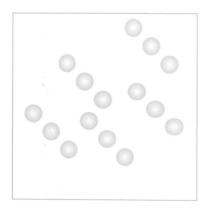

It's easier to remember a sequence of events—each moment leads to the next, triggering a memory. The brain loves patterns, and connections between brain cells are fundamental to its working. It is natural to continue sequences, such as when a child offers to complete a familiar rhyme or we keep track of a movie through the underlying plot.

In the patterns exercise, Box B is easier to manage than Box A. You can glance at Box B for a second, close your eyes, and still count the 15 dots because they are arranged in groups. There is no pattern to Box A—the same information is presented in a manner that is incompatible with the mind. This crucial principle was recorded by Irish mathematician Sir William Hamilton in 1859. He experimented by throwing marbles onto the floor and seeing how long it took him to count them. "If you throw a handful of marbles on the floor, you will find it difficult to view at once more than six or seven at most without confusion," he wrote. "But if you group them in twos, or threes, or fives, you can comprehend as many groups as you can units; because the mind considers these groups as only units." This idea was known as "chunking." The idea of groups is also demonstrated in the word-list exercise. You probably recalled some of the trees in the list since they could be remembered as a group. Memory skills also use connections and divide data into small chunks.

EMOTION

Another word that may have stuck in your mind is famine—a word that provokes an emotional response. As soon as there's a connection

Box B
Left: It's far easier to remember groups of dots, than to remember how many dots there are in a single mass.

between you and the information, it is easier to remember. An extreme example of this is the reputed practice in ancient Greece of taking children to the border between two pieces of land, and spanking them, to create a living record of the boundary line. Their emotions would form a strong lifetime memory.

In the Eight Questions, you're likely to have recalled the weather when you last played a sport because of the emotional cues—the excitement, for example, and your happiness or disappointment at the result. What about remembering an embarrassing moment? This was probably uncomfortably easy. Embarrassment, fear, sadness, and delight are all memory triggers, and can be used as recall strategies.

BRAIN VS. COMPUTER

Human memory is very different from a computer's memory system. Each possesses some important strengths and weaknesses.

In the word list, you probably remembered words at the start because your mind was alert. You probably also recalled some at the end when there was no new information to confuse you. Words near the middle are much harder to recollect—and this is true in any learning situation. With all memory strategies, invest extra time learning

HUMAN MEGABYTES
Right: Your mind and memory put even the most powerful computer in the shade.

the middle sections of information.

Of course, computers don't have this problem and their performance remains constant. It's tempting to regard an electronic memory as superior to a human one. Yet there are occasions in which humans win hands down. In the Eight Questions, you knew the answer to question 3 instantly, and could probably answer question 7 just as easily. Unlike a computer, you didn't need to scroll through all of the numbers stored in your brain to decide that there was no listing for Leonardo da Vinci. General knowledge and common sense told you that. Similarly, there was no need to sort through every word in your mental dictionary to decide that blemf is not a real word. Your mind is very efficient at combining processes and creating shortcuts. These exercises show why the memory succeeds on some occasions, but fails on others.

The exercises in this book will help you use your brain's strengths and make information compatible with the way memory works.

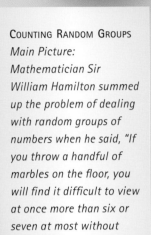

COUNTING RANDOM GROUPS
Main Picture: Mathematician Sir William Hamilton summed up the problem of dealing with random groups of numbers when he said, "If you throw a handful of marbles on the floor, you will find it difficult to view at once more than six or seven at most without confusion."

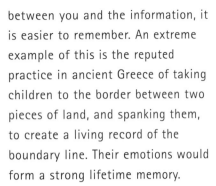

WARMING UP

THIS CHAPTER IS CAREFULLY DESIGNED TO HELP PREPARE YOU FOR THE MEMORY IMPROVEMENTS THAT LIE AHEAD. IT WILL ALSO HELP YOU GET IN THE RIGHT FRAME OF MIND TO USE YOUR BRAIN MORE EFFICIENTLY AND EFFECTIVELY.

GETTING IN THE MOOD

FROM YOUR EXPERIENCES SO FAR, YOU NOW KNOW THAT TO BE
MEMORABLE, INFORMATION MUST SUGGEST VISUAL IMAGES THAT ARE
PATTERNED AND ORGANIZED, UNUSUAL, AND EMOTIONAL. BEAR THESE
POINTS IN MIND WHEN LEARNING YOUR NEW MEMORY TECHNIQUES.

First consider the ways you try to remember things now.
How many of the following memory strategies have you
tried out before?

COMMON MEMORY EXPERIENCES
*Right: Talking on the
telephone is such a fast,
immediate experience, it
often forces us to recall
past events and absorb
new information
simultaneously.*

INFORMATION JUGGLING

You've been given some important
information by telephone, but
you have nowhere to write it
down. You "juggle" names
and numbers, repeating them
aloud as you search your
drawer for the elusive pen
and paper.

MEMORY JOGGERS

You leave yourself physical
reminders of things to do:
notes on the refrigerator,
bags left in the hallway, maybe
even a note on your hand.

NOTING DOWN REMINDERS
*Main Picture: Writing notes is an
effective way of recording
information quickly, but this can
lead to a "lazy" memory.*

MEMORY POSTURES

You perform certain actions when
you're trying to remember, such as
rubbing your neck, scratching your
chin, or folding your arms. These
seem to help you dredge up the
necessary information.

TIP OF THE TONGUE

You're often aware that you know
something, but you can't quite
retrieve the key piece of
information. You know what you
mean, but the right word won't
come, or you recognize someone's
face, but can't put a name to it.

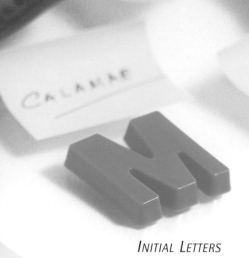

INITIAL LETTERS

When you're struggling with a name, you run through the alphabet in your mind. Does the name begin with A? B? Or was it C . . . ? This often triggers your memory.

REPETITION

To learn new information you read and re-read it, hoping that you eventually remember most of it.

AVOIDANCE TACTICS

You have developed a range of strategies for avoiding the use of your memory. You rely on others to remember important information for you; you're reluctant to learn new skills; and you avoid using people's names in case you get them wrong.

Sound familiar? Memory can certainly seem capricious, and most of us have to struggle to make it do what we want. Ironically, part of the problem is the very power of the memory. You recognize a face instantly, for example, but can't quite connect it with a name. You know the right word, but it won't come to mind immediately. Our memories work phenomenally well most of the time, so it's frustrating when they appear to let us down.

Although few people would make a conscious effort to use memory techniques, the strategies mentioned here demonstrate that we all have various ways to make remembering easier. This book will help you to use the most effective methods ever developed—tried, tested, and proved effective again and again since the days of ancient Greece. Begin by banishing the words "I forgot," because you *can* remember everything you want once you start using your brain the way it was originally designed to be used.

SUCCESSFUL THINKING

STAY CALM

Main Picture: Your memory capacity decreases as your anxiety level rises. This is especially apparent when you are learning information by heart, for such anxious moments as wedding speeches and work presentations. But if you can keep your emotions under control, you're halfway there!

POSITIVE THINKING IS IMPORTANT WHATEVER YOU'RE TRYING TO DO, BUT IT IS ABSOLUTELY ESSENTIAL WHEN YOU'RE USING YOUR MEMORY.

How many times have you told yourself and others that you have a terrible memory? In the short time you've been reading this book, though, you've proved that your memory works perfectly well. If you think that you're not young or clever enough to improve your old techniques, keep in mind that it takes bravery to step out of the comfort zone and stretch your mental boundaries, but the rewards can be life-changing.

NERVOUS ENERGY

Memory and nerves are closely linked. When you're anxious, remembering becomes a major challenge. Imagine you are about to give a speech at a wedding. Your heart is racing, your palms are sweating, and your memory probably seems out of control.

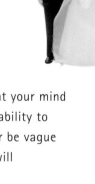

If you'd learned to use your memory, the scene would be different. Memory techniques give you the assurance that your mind is going to do what you want. Your ability to summon information will no longer be vague and unpredictable. Instead, you will deliberately invest time making information memorable, knowing exactly what you need to do to recall it. Having a good memory makes you feel more confident, and that confidence brings rewards of its own—at work and in your social life.

A word of caution, though: Keep your goals within reach. If you force yourself to try too much, too fast, you'll start out convinced you're going to fail—so, invariably, you will. That experience increases your sense of limitation, so your confidence plummets further, and you become less likely to seek challenges.

In the sport of weightlifting, 500 pounds (226.8kg) was long regarded as a near-impossible target. Vasily Alexeyev had several times come close to the magic 500-pound (226.8kg) mark, without success. One day, his trainers challenged him to match his own world record of 499.9 pounds (226.75kg) —which he did without a problem. What Alexeyev didn't realize until after he had lowered the bar, was that he had actually raised 501.5 pounds (227.5kg)—the trainers had surreptitiously added 1.6 extra pounds (0.73kg). The barrier was broken: A few years later, at the 1976 Olympic Games, Alexeyev lifted 564 pounds (255.8kg).

Rigid notions about our

RELAX:
YOU CAN DO IT
Below: If you are physically and mentally relaxed, you will be in a better position to set realistic goals for maximizing your memory.

own limitations hold us back from achieving our full potential. In contrast, the memory techniques outlined in this book operate in the realm of the imagination, where anything is possible. They unleash your imagination, so that you can visualize success. They also put you in the right frame of mind to tackle any mental challenge. Rather than admonishing you to "be confident," they give you the means to go beyond your self-imposed limits.

RELAXATION

The first step is to relax and to focus on the task at hand. Imagination is the key to relaxation as well as memory, so get ready to loosen the reins on your mind.

Picture yourself in your ultimate relaxation zone. If you suddenly could be transported to the most relaxing spot on earth or beyond, where would you go? Spend a couple of minutes just luxuriating in the restful quality of this place.

How good was your imagination? You may have found this exercise difficult, but it's a prelude to relaxing on the exercises to come. There will be more chances to practice using your imagination along the way.

IMAGINATION PRACTICE

MAKE SURE YOU'RE COMFORTABLE. THE SECRET OF GOOD
MEMORY IS MAKING MEMORY EASY, SO DON'T NEGLECT
PRACTICALITIES, SUCH AS POSTURE AND SURROUNDINGS. IS
YOUR CHOSEN CHAIR SUITABLE? WHAT ABOUT THE TEMPERATURE
IN THE ROOM, OR THE LEVEL OF NOISE? GOOD VISUALIZATION
IS DIFFICULT IF YOU'RE DISTRACTED.

PICTURE THIS

Your task is to visualize a regular
cardboard box. Let your mind go
blank, then picture this box in your
mind's eye. Next, imagine walking
around the box, looking at it from
different angles. See yourself lifting
the box and turning it over,
concentrating on what it looks like
from every perspective. Give the box
a color. How does the color make
you feel? Memories are linked with
how we feel about what we're
learning, so it always makes sense
to focus on every emotional
response. Think of touching the box.
Give it an imagined texture,
pleasant or unpleasant. Does the box
have a smell? If you tap it, what
noise does it make? Imagine taking
a bite out of it. What would a
mouthful of this box be like?

Your imagination can give memorable detail to the most mundane items. You can also exaggerate images, make them surreal—even bring them to life.

Now picture a car—no ordinary automobile, but the most expensive model in the world. What color is it? What gadgets does it possess? How does it look, sound, and smell when it's moving? Next, picture a tree. The unusual thing about this tree is that it can walk and talk. Imagine you're an animator: How does a walking tree move, and what sound does it make when it talks?

TRANSFORMATIONS
Your imagination can also transform one thing into another. Picture the car again—and use your skills of visualization to turn it into. . . an elephant. Make the transformation gradually. Perhaps it starts with the mirrors turning into huge ears. Each wheel could break off to reveal a leg. The steering wheel might turn into a trunk and the exhaust could become the elephant's tail.

VIEWING FROM EVERY ANGLE
Left: When exercising your imagination, you need to create your own mental virtual reality zone, in which your visualization techniques are so effective, you feel as if you are actually experiencing the event.

CREATING MENTAL PICTURES

YOUR IMAGINATION ALLOWS YOU TO TAKE CONTROL OF INFORMATION AND DO WHAT YOU WANT WITH IT. TO PRACTICE THIS SKILL, TRY TO IMAGINE DESTROYING EACH OF THE OBJECTS SHOWN BELOW IN A WAY THAT'S PARTICULARLY STRIKING—PULL THE SPRING OUT OF THE CLOCK, OR DROP THE CHINA PIG FROM A TOWER.

clock   china pig   book   toy duck   shell

fish tank   glass   cup   bauble   boot

lamp   chair   iron   clothes   television

WHEN YOU'VE IMAGINED DESTROYING THE 15 OBJECTS, COVER THE IMAGES. PRINTED BELOW IS A SECOND SET OF IMAGES, CONTAINING 12 OF THE OBJECTS AND THREE NEW ONES. CAN YOU PICK OUT THE THREE THAT YOU DIDN'T DESTROY?

ONCE YOU'VE MADE A CONNECTION WITH INFORMATION, IT BECOMES EASY TO REMEMBER IT. YOU SHOULDN'T HAVE ANY DIFFICULTY SPOTTING THE NEW IMAGES IN THE SECOND SET, SINCE YOU HAD NO MEMORY OF INTERACTING WITH THEM.

LEARNING TO FORGET

POSSIBLY THE BEST MEMORY EVER TESTED BELONGED TO
SHERESHEVSKY, THE RESEARCH SUBJECT OF THE GREAT RUSSIAN
PSYCHOLOGIST, ALEXANDER LURIA. IT APPEARED THAT SHERESHEVSKY
NEVER FORGOT ANYTHING. HE COULD READ A COMPLEX FORMULA JUST
ONCE, AND RECALL IT YEARS LATER. HE REMEMBERED PAGES OF TEXT EXACTLY.
GIVEN A VAST GRID OF RANDOM NUMBERS, HE COULD REEL THEM OFF IN MINUTES.

Shereshevsky had a condition known as synesthesia, where the senses appear to overlap. Information came to him with a range of details. In his mind, names had colors, numbers had smells, words had texture. He was alive with responses. Nothing was abstract—and so nothing was forgotten.

Shereshevsky remembered too much, and he had to teach himself to forget by imagining writing unwanted data on sheets of paper, then setting fire to them. This made the information uniform and abstract, and less likely to stick in his mind. The way most of us are taught to remember—by taking notes— was the best way to forget.

INFORMATION OVERLOAD

Imagination-based memory skills focus on remembering exactly what you need to know, and forgetting it when it's not required. Using your imagination, you just slot in the data, then remove it.

THE CYCLE OF SUCCESS

Take another trip to your relaxation zone. This time, utilize everything you've learned so far to get the most out of the experience. Draw on all your senses, the way you did earlier in the licking-the-lemon scenario. Visualize the images, sounds, and sensations that will help you focus.

Take yourself back to your most relaxing place. Imagine turning full circle to survey the entire scene before choosing one viewpoint. Decide how you're sitting and how each part of your body feels. How warm is it? Is there a breeze? What can you hear and smell? How does it feel?

Let your mind and body relax as you bring this scene to life. The power of your imagination will, overall, place you in a cycle of success to meet the challenges ahead.

PROGRESS TEST TWO

USE YOUR STATE OF RELAXATION TO FOCUS IN ON THE FOLLOWING EXERCISES.

WORD LIST

READ THE LIST OF WORDS PRINTED HERE,
SPENDING A COUPLE OF SECONDS ON EACH
ONE. AS YOU GO THROUGH THE LIST, CREATE
A MENTAL PICTURE OF EACH OBJECT, USING
THE IMAGES ABOVE EACH WORD AS A
TRIGGER. EXAGGERATE THEM; MAKE THEM
HUGE, TINY, STRANGELY SHAPED, BRIGHTLY
COLORED. CALL ON YOUR OTHER SENSES AND
TAP INTO YOUR EMOTIONS TO BRING EACH
WORD TO LIFE.

AS SOON AS YOU FINISH THE LIST, TURN THE
PAGE TO TEST YOURSELF.

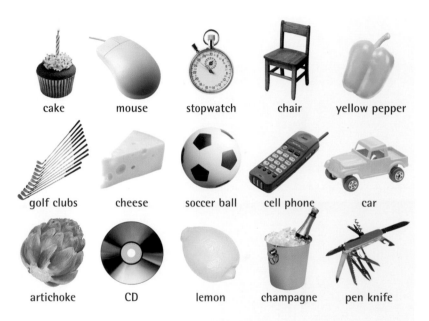

cake	mouse	stopwatch	chair	yellow pepper
golf clubs	cheese	soccer ball	cell phone	car
artichoke	CD	lemon	champagne	pen knife

WORD PAIRS

THIS EXERCISE TESTS YOUR ABILITY TO REMEMBER PAIRS OF
WORDS. USE YOUR IMAGINATION TO VISUALIZE EACH WORD IN AS
MANY WAYS AS POSSIBLE—BUT CONNECT THE TWO WORDS IN
EACH PAIR. THERE ARE NO VISUAL TRIGGERS THIS TIME, SO YOU
HAVE TO WORK A LITTLE HARDER.

YOU COULD PICTURE THEM LINKED IN A STRANGE WAY, OR RESTING
ON TOP OF EACH OTHER. YOU COULD VISUALIZE ONE EXPLODING TO
RELEASE THE OTHER, OR THE FIRST MORPHING INTO THE SECOND.
ONCE YOU'VE READ THROUGH THE LIST WITH THIS FOCUS, TURN
THE PAGE TO CHECK HOW WELL YOU'VE DONE.

CD	briefcase	cushion
lettuce	paint	peas
nail	boot	castle
bag	swan	chocolate
hair	watch	milk
pencil	camera	staircase
moon	snake	bush
hand	sandwich	baby
stage	bicycle	trailer
sea	tape	necktie

HOW WELL DID YOU DO?

NOW IS YOUR CHANCE TO SEE HOW MUCH PROGRESS YOU HAVE MADE. STAY CALM, AND THE INFORMATION WILL FLOW EASILY. IF YOUR MIND GOES BLANK, TAKE A BREAK, THEN START AGAIN.

WORD LIST

HOW MANY OF THE 15 WORDS CAN YOU REMEMBER? WRITE THEM DOWN IN ANY ORDER. AS YOU DO THIS EXERCISE, FOCUS ON THE MOMENT WHEN EACH WORD RETURNS TO YOUR MIND AND HOW IT MAKES YOU FEEL. WITH TIME, RECAPTURING MEMORIES CAN BE AS NATURAL AS CATCHING A BALL.

....
....
....
....
....
....
....
....
....
....
....
....
....
....
....

WORD PAIRS

WRITE DOWN AS MANY OF THE THE WORD PAIRS AS YOU CAN, AND SEE HOW IT FEELS WHEN THEY COME BACK TO YOU. NEXT, TRY A DIFFERENT VERSION OF THE TEST. PRINTED BELOW ARE THE FIRST WORDS FROM EACH PAIR—JUST WRITE DOWN THE SECOND WORD.

briefcase   ....
boot   ....
watch   ....
snake   ....
bicycle   ....
CD   ....
nail   ....
hair   ....
moon   ....
stage   ....
cushion   ....
castle   ....
milk   ....
bush   ....
trailer   ....

Tom's Story

READ THIS STORY THROUGH ONCE. YOU WILL BE TESTED ON IT LATER IN THE BOOK.

It was Saturday morning and Tom headed downtown to buy some milk. He parked his car, then took the elevator to the first floor. His first destination was the bank, where he withdrew some cash. Next he went to a photo-store to pick up his vacation pictures and some new film. He'd spent a week in Paris, and his favorite shots were of the Eiffel Tower, the Arc de Triomphe, and Notre Dame.

Tom then walked to a bookstore to look for information on his favorite subjects: sailing and fine art. He was in luck, because there was a new book about oceangoing yachts, as well as the latest biography of Leonardo da Vinci, with the Mona Lisa on the cover. He bought them both, along with a travel guide to Japan, his next foreign destination, where he was scheduled to attend a conference.

Tom stopped for a cup of coffee and a sandwich, and he did the crossword in the daily paper, periodically. Finally he went to an electronics store to buy new batteries for his electronic organizer. While he was there he browsed among the computers and talked to a sales clerk about the latest software.

RECAP

EXERCISING YOUR MEMORY IS LIKE A PHYSICAL
WORKOUT, IN THAT BOTH SHOULD BEGIN WITH A
WARM-UP. WITH YOUR MIND, THIS MEANS
LEARNING TO RELAX.

IMPROVING YOUR MEMORY WILL, in the long run, have a
positive effect on your overall well-being. You will have
new-found confidence, positive thoughts, and freedom
from anxiety. Once you are in control of your mind, no
vital piece of information will ever again elude you.

Start the journey to maximized memory by learning to
relax. Only when you are stress- and tension-free can you
give your imagination absolute free rein. Imagination and
visualization are essential to a good memory, because
they link feelings or images to abstract information. Fully
relaxed visualization employs all the senses and draws on
your emotions to make a strong connection between the
sterile information and the lively imagery you create
around it. The more relaxed you are, the greater your
capacity to exaggerate imagery will be, making it all the
more memorable.

MEMORY
BUILDING

GREAT CONFIDENCE COMES WHEN YOU UNDERSTAND THE WAY YOUR MEMORY WORKS AND KNOW HOW TO ORGANIZE YOUR THINKING ALONG THE RIGHT LINES. JUST AS A VAST ENCYCLOPEDIA OR DESK TRAY IS DIVIDED INTO MANAGEABLE SECTIONS, SO YOUR MEMORY CAN STORE DATA IN DEFINED AREAS. KNOW HOW YOUR MIND WORKS BEST AND YOU CAN BUILD A STRUCTURED MEMORY.

INTRODUCING FRAMEWORKS

FEELING RELAXED, FOCUSED, AND CONFIDENT, YOU ARE NOW AWARE OF THE POWER OF YOUR IMAGINATION AND READY TO CONSTRUCT THE MENTAL FRAMEWORKS THAT WILL HELP YOU REMEMBER. ONCE YOU'RE COMFORTABLE WITH THESE FRAMEWORKS, YOU CAN FILL THEM WITH ANY KIND OF INFORMATION.

THINK SPATIALLY
Below: The world globe is an accessible entry point to the idea of mental maps.

We all impose mental frameworks on the world around us. Consider the village, town, or city where you live. What is your mental map of it like? If you make a particular journey regularly, your map is probably constructed around that route. The shape of your mental map, the distances within it, and its orientation in your mind all depend on your experiences and priorities. Other people will have different concepts of the same place, depending on the routes they take, the places they visit, and the areas they first became acquainted with.

SPATIAL THINKING

It is natural to remember spatially. Many people find it easy to remember where a certain passage appears in a book, even if they can't remember the exact words in the passage. They can sometimes even

VISUALIZING NUMBERS

Main Picture : It is sometimes easier to process numeric information by visualizing the actual numbers in your mind—maybe lined up horizontally or written down on paper.

picture the page in question and say whether a certain piece of information is on the left or right, at the top or bottom, in a box or spread out. Perhaps you can describe how you see information in your mind's eye. Some people visualize numbers in a particular spatial formation: one to 10 running horizontally, for example, then 10 to 20 climbing vertically, turning right, or forming an arc.

The idea of using spatial thinking to boost the memory goes back as far as ancient Greece. Legend has it that a huge dinner party was being given by a magnate named Scopas, when the roof of his mansion collapsed, burying hundreds of guests under piles of rubble. There was just one survivor, a famous poet named Simonides of Ceos, and he proved able to recall the identity of every one of the victims. Because he had trained his memory, he could picture the dining-hall in his mind's eye and recall each guest from the position in which he or she had been sitting. He was accustomed to creating mental frameworks to remember his poetry, and he was able to put his mind to good use.

MENTAL FRAMEWORKS

The Romans turned this principle into a specific memory system, often referred to as the "Roman Room" technique. Romans from many walks of life appear to have used a book titled *Ad Herennium*, which showed how mental frameworks could hold all the information they needed.

By the time of the Renaissance, the system had acquired a theatrical twist. Philosopher and playwright Giulio Camillo devised a mental "memory theater" in which the audience stood on the stage and looked out toward rows of props arranged in memorable patterns. Camillo is said to have created numerous mental buildings decorated with images to help him recall vast amounts of information.

It's been suggested that the design of Shakespeare's Globe theater was intended to boost the memory. In Shakespeare's day, an audience needed to follow sometimes complicated plots for several hours, with little scenery, few props, and simple costumes to prompt their memory. It was important for the theater to provide a clear framework for the play. Different characters appeared and reappeared from particular parts of the theater, and various areas of the building came to represent themes in the drama.

Learning to create your own mental frameworks can revolutionize your life. Frameworks allow you to store and recall the information you need and boost your performance in all kinds of endeavors. Building a structured memory means using the way your mind works naturally to start remembering with ease.

ELECTRONIC FRAMEWORKS

Right: Electronic circuitry illustrates an idealized view of well-ordered information. Each function has its own defined area on the board, and can be expanded or reduced as required.

BUILDING BASIC FRAMEWORKS

Mental frameworks can be modeled on buildings, walks, or journeys that you know well. Choose your neighborhood office building, regular shopping area, or a memorable vacation site. The aim is to use a familiar framework to hold new information.

Every framework should have 10 areas, each as different from the others as possible. If the site on which you base your framework has more than 10 areas, simply highlight 10 that you can remember.

The route from area to area needs to be absolutely clear. It often helps to sketch the path as you design it, just to be sure how it will take shape in your mind. Always choose the most obvious route so that you'll never have difficulty negotiating it quickly.

Once you're sure of the 10 areas and know the route from one to 10, fill each part of the framework with images. The images can remind you of names, words, numbers, ideas, rules, jobs, directions—every kind of information you need. To retrieve a piece of information, simply take a mental journey back through the 10 areas, rediscovering all the picture clues you left behind.

The following pages feature two examples of the framework technique in practice. Try using these ready-made frameworks to learn the information they contain. You'll need to fire your imagination and make the data compatible with the way your mind works. Concentrate on giving all the pictures as much vivid detail as possible, and bring in your emotions. How would you feel if you really entered these places and experienced such weird happenings?

A CHILD'S FRAMEWORK

Below: A dollhouse is a perfect example of a framework model: each room is designed with a specific function and is filled with items suited to the use of the space. When children play with a dollhouse year after year, the layout and contents of the house become embedded in their memory.

FRAMEWORK EXAMPLE

These two examples show Framework B: The Office. The composite framework (above) shows all the rooms ready to be used for a specific memory challenge. The framework in action (below) shows an individual room awaiting some information to be slotted in. In this case, the boss's office is the place where you will remember ice cream and dishwashing detergent. A suggested narrative (see pages 62–63) provides the link between the framework and the information.

TO USE EACH FRAMEWORK

Read the descriptions of the 10 areas for each framework, then spend a few minutes walking through them in your mind to familiarize yourself with the layout. When you start creating your own frameworks, this process will be done entirely by imagination. Check that you're comfortable with the route by moving through it backwards, from area 10 to area one. When you're familiar with the basic framework, read how the information is turned into images and how the framework changes in action. Fix the pictures into place, immerse yourself in the journey, and you'll be amazed at how easily you remember information.

THE COMPOSITE FRAMEWORK

THE FRAMEWORK IN ACTION

9 YOUR BOSS'S OFFICE

Ice Cream and Dishwashing Detergent
Your boss is too busy to see you because he's eating an ice cream. As soon as he's finished, he washes his hands with powerful dishwashing detergent, and the bubbles fill his luxurious office.

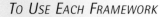

FRAMEWORK A: THE HOUSE

THIS FRAMEWORK USES AN IMAGINATIVE NARRATIVE TO HELP YOU REMEMBER A LIST OF SPORTS. THE HOUSE IS DIVIDED INTO **10** AREAS, AND THE FIRST STAGE IS TO GET TO KNOW THE INTERIOR LAYOUT.

10 **THE NURSERY**
Your journey ends in the nursery, which contains a large playpen full of soft toys. The walls are painted in bright, stimulating colors.

1 **THE FRONT DOOR**
This is where your mental journey begins. You're standing in front of a heavy oak door with a polished brass knocker in the center. Try it; imagine the noise it would make. The door itself creaks loudly as you open it and enter the house.

2 **THE HALLWAY**
Does the hall feel warm or cold? Check your appearance in the long mirror on the wall, then use one of the pegs to hang up your coat. Take off your shoes before walking into . . .

3 **THE LIVING ROOM**
The carpet here is luxurious. Imagine how it feels under your feet. You can make yourself comfortable here for a few minutes, spreading out on the soft couch. Look around you: Is the room decorated to your taste? Do you like the huge oil-painting that's hanging over the fire?

4 **THE DINING ROOM**
This next stopping-point has a huge mahogany table, set for a large banquet, at its center. Where would you like to sit? To find out what food you might be served, take a leisurely walk into . . .

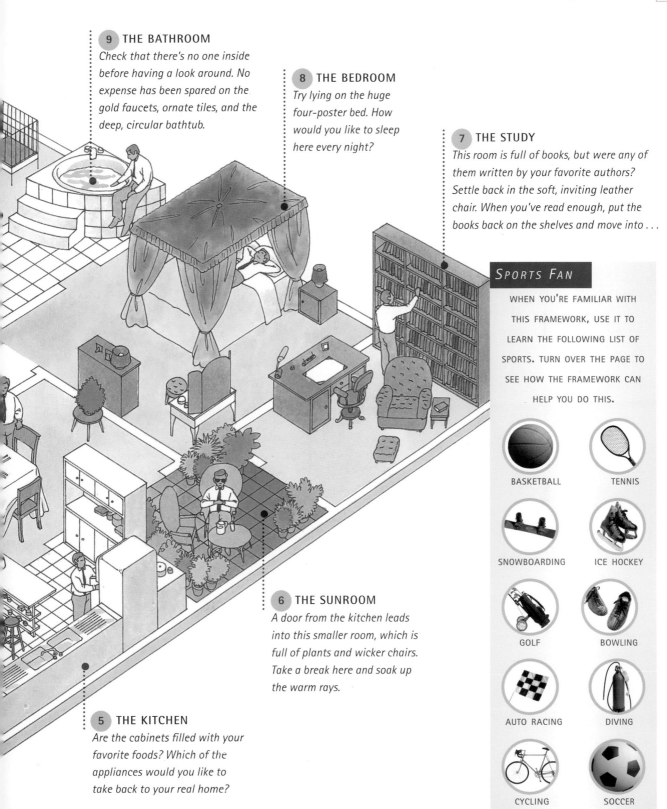

9 THE BATHROOM
Check that there's no one inside before having a look around. No expense has been spared on the gold faucets, ornate tiles, and the deep, circular bathtub.

8 THE BEDROOM
Try lying on the huge four-poster bed. How would you like to sleep here every night?

7 THE STUDY
This room is full of books, but were any of them written by your favorite authors? Settle back in the soft, inviting leather chair. When you've read enough, put the books back on the shelves and move into . . .

SPORTS FAN

WHEN YOU'RE FAMILIAR WITH THIS FRAMEWORK, USE IT TO LEARN THE FOLLOWING LIST OF SPORTS. TURN OVER THE PAGE TO SEE HOW THE FRAMEWORK CAN HELP YOU DO THIS.

BASKETBALL

TENNIS

SNOWBOARDING

ICE HOCKEY

GOLF

BOWLING

AUTO RACING

DIVING

CYCLING

SOCCER

6 THE SUNROOM
A door from the kitchen leads into this smaller room, which is full of plants and wicker chairs. Take a break here and soak up the warm rays.

5 THE KITCHEN
Are the cabinets filled with your favorite foods? Which of the appliances would you like to take back to your real home?

SLOTTING IN THE INFORMATION

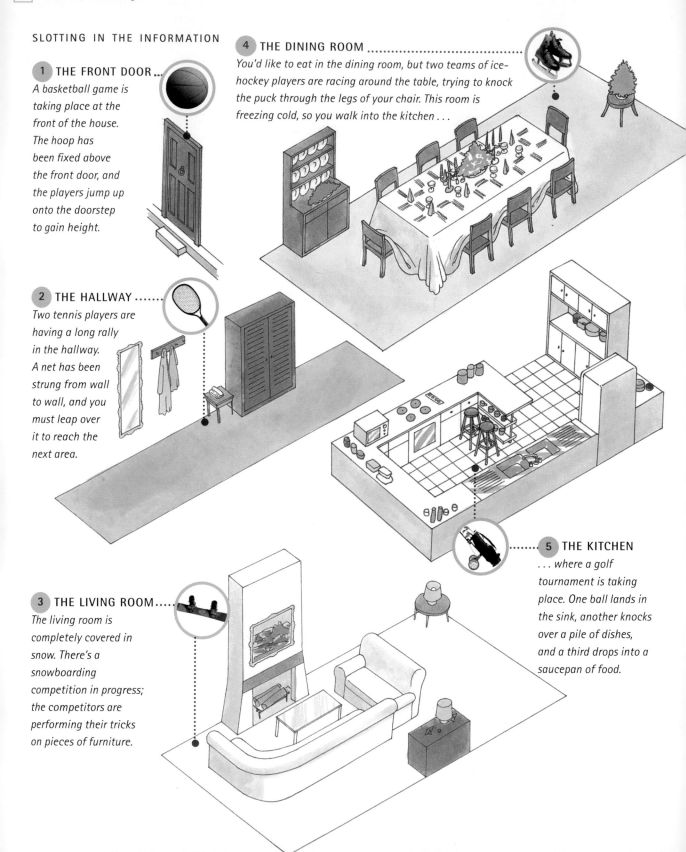

1 THE FRONT DOOR...

A basketball game is taking place at the front of the house. The hoop has been fixed above the front door, and the players jump up onto the doorstep to gain height.

4 THE DINING ROOM ....

You'd like to eat in the dining room, but two teams of ice-hockey players are racing around the table, trying to knock the puck through the legs of your chair. This room is freezing cold, so you walk into the kitchen . . .

2 THE HALLWAY ....

Two tennis players are having a long rally in the hallway. A net has been strung from wall to wall, and you must leap over it to reach the next area.

5 THE KITCHEN

. . . where a golf tournament is taking place. One ball lands in the sink, another knocks over a pile of dishes, and a third drops into a saucepan of food.

3 THE LIVING ROOM ....

The living room is completely covered in snow. There's a snowboarding competition in progress; the competitors are performing their tricks on pieces of furniture.

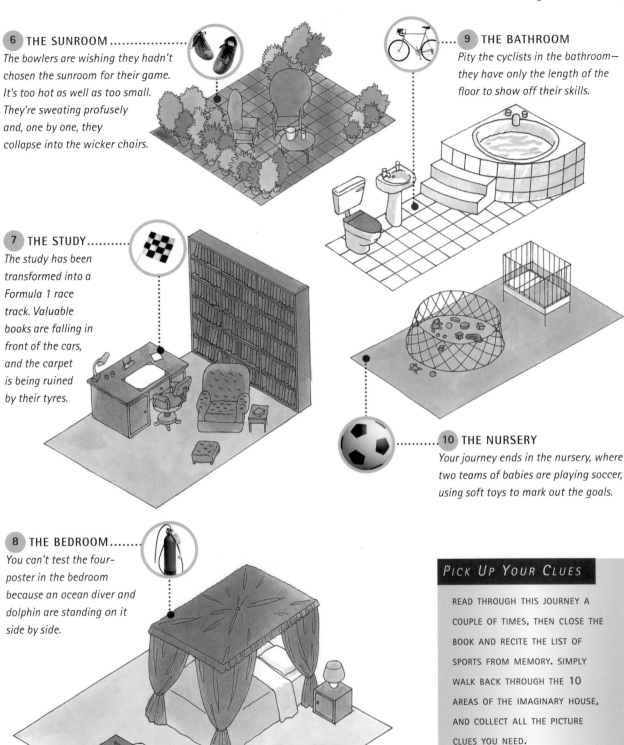

6 THE SUNROOM ....

The bowlers are wishing they hadn't chosen the sunroom for their game. It's too hot as well as too small. They're sweating profusely and, one by one, they collapse into the wicker chairs.

7 THE STUDY ....

The study has been transformed into a Formula 1 race track. Valuable books are falling in front of the cars, and the carpet is being ruined by their tyres.

8 THE BEDROOM ....

You can't test the four-poster in the bedroom because an ocean diver and dolphin are standing on it side by side.

9 THE BATHROOM

Pity the cyclists in the bathroom— they have only the length of the floor to show off their skills.

10 THE NURSERY

Your journey ends in the nursery, where two teams of babies are playing soccer, using soft toys to mark out the goals.

PICK UP YOUR CLUES

READ THROUGH THIS JOURNEY A COUPLE OF TIMES, THEN CLOSE THE BOOK AND RECITE THE LIST OF SPORTS FROM MEMORY. SIMPLY WALK BACK THROUGH THE 10 AREAS OF THE IMAGINARY HOUSE, AND COLLECT ALL THE PICTURE CLUES YOU NEED.

FRAMEWORK B: THE OFFICE

REMEMBERING A LONGER LIST: THIS FRAMEWORK ALSO
CONSISTS OF **10** DISTINCT AREAS IN A FAMILIAR PLACE.
USE YOUR IMAGINATION TO BRING THE JOURNEY TO LIFE
AS YOU MOVE FROM ROOM TO ROOM.

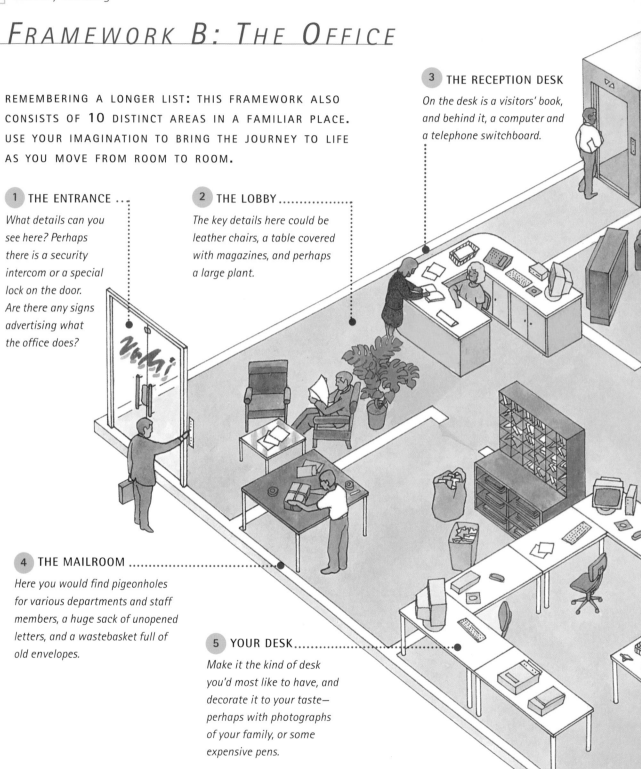

3 THE RECEPTION DESK

*On the desk is a visitors' book,
and behind it, a computer and
a telephone switchboard.*

1 THE ENTRANCE

*What details can you
see here? Perhaps
there is a security
intercom or a special
lock on the door.
Are there any signs
advertising what
the office does?*

2 THE LOBBY

*The key details here could be
leather chairs, a table covered
with magazines, and perhaps
a large plant.*

4 THE MAILROOM

*Here you would find pigeonholes
for various departments and staff
members, a huge sack of unopened
letters, and a wastebasket full of
old envelopes.*

5 YOUR DESK

*Make it the kind of desk
you'd most like to have, and
decorate it to your taste—
perhaps with photographs
of your family, or some
expensive pens.*

10 THE ELEVATOR

Imagine ending your journey by taking the elevator out of the building. What sounds does it make? Are there any notices to tell you what to do if it jams?

9 YOUR BOSS'S OFFICE

Make this a vast, sumptuous room, with plenty of status symbols: huge television, antique desk, expensive leather couches.

8 THE RESTROOM

Concentrate on how this room looks and smells, and highlight sensory details such as the soap dispenser and the hand drier.

7 THE WATER COOLER

Use your imagination to make the water ultra cool and fresh. Taste the water to check that the machine is worth the investment.

6 THE PHOTOCOPIER

Perhaps this is an old model that works poorly. What noise does it make when you eventually get it to print?

WEEKLY GROCERIES

USE THE FRAMEWORK TO LEARN THIS LIST OF GROCERIES. SEE OVERLEAF FOR A SUGGESTED NARRATIVE.

WINE

BREAD

CORN

CABBAGE

PINEAPPLE

BLOOD ORANGE

GRAPES

SHRIMP

COFFEE

APPLE

TOMATO

DONUT

TURKEY

MUSHROOMS

BANANAS

RICE

ICE CREAM

DISHWASHING DETERGENT

POTATOES

POPCORN

SLOTTING IN THE INFORMATION: WITH A LONGER LIST OF ITEMS TO REMEMBER, YOU REALLY HAVE TO CONCENTRATE ON WEAVING THEM INTO THE FRAMEWORK NARRATIVE. USE THIS STORY TO GET YOU GOING.

1 THE ENTRANCE

Wine and Bread

Wine is seeping from under the office door, which seems to be made of bread.

4 THE MAILROOM

Grapes and Shrimp

Grapes have been pushed into every pigeon hole in the mailroom. The mailbag is crammed to overflowing with shrimps.

5 YOUR DESK

Coffee and Apple

Your desk is completely clear except for two items: a large, steaming cup of coffee, and a shiny red apple.

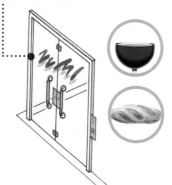

2 THE LOBBY

Corn and Cabbage

A huge corn cob is sitting in the lobby. The floor here is tiled with hundreds of cabbage leaves.

6 THE WATER COOLER

Tomato and Donut

When you put your cup under the spout, something strange comes out: a tomato. You also notice a donut bobbing around in the water canister.

3 THE RECEPTION DESK

Pineapple and Blood Orange

A pineapple is working as the office receptionist. The reception desk itself is half a blood orange.

8 **THE PHOTOCOPIER**

Bananas and Rice

At the photocopier, someone is trying to copy a banana—but the machine has malfunctioned, and rice is pouring out instead.

7 **THE RESTROOM**

Turkey and Mushrooms

There's a turkey running around in the restroom. It's not a pleasant place to be, because the walls are covered with large mushrooms.

10 **THE ELEVATOR**

Potatoes and Popcorn

To ride the elevator, you must squeeze between two large piles of potatoes. The floor of the elevator is covered with popcorn, which crunches noisily under your feet.

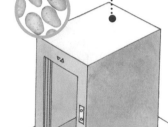

9 **YOUR BOSS'S OFFICE**

Ice Cream and Dishwashing Detergent

Your boss is too busy to see you because he's eating an ice cream. As soon as he's finished, he washes his hands with powerful dishwashing detergent, and the bubbles fill his luxurious office.

TEST YOURSELF

EACH OF THE **10** ROOMS NOW CONTAINS TWO ITEMS FROM THE LIST. RUN THROUGH THE JOURNEY ONCE MORE, THEN CLOSE THE BOOK AND SEE HOW MANY OF THE **20** ITEMS YOU REMEMBER TO BUY.

PROGRESS TEST THREE

TO COMPLETE THIS TEST, FIRST DESIGN YOUR OWN MENTAL
FRAMEWORK OR USE ONE OF THE EXAMPLES GIVEN EARLIER.

FRAMEWORK BASICS

HERE'S A REMINDER

OF THE KEY STEPS:

- Pick a place you know very well.
- Divide it into 10 distinct areas.
- Choose a route from area one to area 10.
- Sketch the route if necessary.
- Visualize yourself walking the route.
- Walk the route in reverse to check that it's clear in your mind.

WHEN YOUR FRAMEWORK IS IN PLACE, USE IT TO LEARN THE FOLLOWING LIST:

rabbit   cake   shell   coffee   nail

radio   watch   idea   happiness   doll

REMEMBERING LISTS

TO MEMORIZE A

LIST USING A FRAMEWORK:

- Pick a place you know well.
- Give each item on the list a vivid picture.
- Fix a picture or pictures into each of the 10 areas.
- Use your imagination to make each scene memorable.
- Exaggerate the images to make them unusual and vivid.
- Involve all your senses.
- Imagine how you'd react if the events really were taking place.

NEXT, DOUBLE THE AMOUNT OF INFORMATION CONTAINED IN YOUR MEMORY ROUTE.

ADD A SECOND ITEM TO EACH AREA, CONNECTING IT IN SOME WAY WITH THE FIRST.

THE SECOND PART OF THE LIST IS AS FOLLOWS:

ball   contentment   paint   ring   balloon

chocolate   bell   phone   chair   depression

RECAP

THE MIND NATURALLY IMPOSES FRAMEWORKS ON
THE WORLD TO GIVE INFORMATION ORDER AND
SHAPE. CONSIDER YOUR OWN MENTAL MAPS
AROUND BUILDINGS, TOWNS, AND COUNTRIES. HOW
DO YOU ARRANGE DATA IN YOUR MENTAL FIELD?

IN ANCIENT TIMES, philosophers and thinkers used connections between place and memory, locating points on a mental journey to remember information. You can take a similar journey by creating your own memory framework. The technique involves choosing a place you know well (your home, for example), dividing it into specific areas, and imagining a journey through those areas, concentrating on the details or the hooks on which images can be hung.

Then work on putting your framework into use by mentally placing a specific image in each area and creating a strong connection between each image and the place in which it has been fixed. The secret to success is to bring in as many senses and feelings as possible, creating a whole scene that cannot be forgotten. Then retrace your steps to recall the images, discovering the item you've located in each area.

TOTAL RECALL

ARMED WITH BASIC MEMORY PRINCIPLES,

YOU CAN START TO FOCUS YOUR MIND ON

HARD INFORMATION AND WORK TO MAKE IT

MEMORABLE. ANY SORT OF MATERIAL CAN

BE DIVIDED INTO MANAGEABLE CHUNKS

AND ASSIGNED A REMINDER IMAGE. THESE

IMAGES CAN BE SLOTTED INTO MENTAL

FRAMEWORKS TO HELP YOU RECALL THE

INFORMATION QUICKLY AND ON DEMAND.

START MAKING EVERYTHING IN YOUR LIFE

COMPATIBLE WITH THE WAY YOUR MIND

WORKS AND YOU WON'T FORGET A THING.

USING YOUR IMAGINATION

IMAGINATION IS AT THE HEART OF ALL GOOD MEMORY STRATEGIES, ALLOWING YOU TO CREATE MENTAL PICTURES THAT GIVE YOU ACCESS TO ANY INFORMATION YOU NEED TO RECALL. BECAUSE A SIMPLE PICTURE CAN TRIGGER COMPLICATED MEMORIES, THESE TECHNIQUES ARE ESPECIALLY POWERFUL.

YOU DON'T NEED LUCK

Main Picture: The horseshoe is a traditional symbol of luck, but with your new improved memory systems, you can be sure you won't need it . . . especially if you are giving the equestrian talk described here.

A picture can represent any body of information, making it both manageable and memorable. You already retain huge amounts of data without any difficulty. Frequently, therefore, all your brain needs is a quick reminder. Actors on stage need a prompt from time to time, but once they have the next few words in a speech, they can carry on unaided. Likewise, your brain will recall large chunks of information when triggered by a simple picture.

Think of these images as picture clues. They are simplified versions of the original material, but memorable enough to bring all the details back to your mind.

Suppose you have to give a talk on horseback riding for beginners. Even though you know your subject well, you will benefit from a set of ordered picture clues to help you

speak with fluency and confidence. To remember each in sequence, the trick is to think up a memorable picture to represent every point. Those pictures will slot into place in a memory framework, enabling you to recall all the important parts of your talk with ease, and in the correct order.

BREAK DOWN THE DATA

Planning the talk, you might jot down the following main points:

1   costs
2   different breeds
3   clothing
4   equipment
5   mounting/dismounting
6   teachers
7   food
8   caring for horses' hooves
9   safe transport
10 competitions

Decide on suitable images, then choose a familiar memory framework and fix
an image into place in each of the ten areas. For example, if you choose
Framework A: The House, your visualized journey starts at the front door . . .

. . . where you find five-dollar bills nailed around the door frame. Several
types of horses are galloping through the hallway. Riding clothes are spread
out on the sofa in the living room. Expensive equipment is lying on the
dining-room table. The kitchen is full of ladders. A teacher you remember
from school is relaxing in the sunroom. Buckets of oats are spilling across the
floor of the study. In the bedroom, a horse trailer is standing where the bed
should be. There's an automobile floating in the bath. Finally, the crib in the
nursery is completely covered with rosettes.

To give your talk, wander back through the framework, finding a picture clue
in each area. Each picture prompts you to say everything in the right order.

ASSIGN PICTURE CLUES

Here are examples of some of the picture clues you might choose.

1 costs:
large dollar bills.

2 different
breeds: images of
the horses
themselves, with
a range of sizes
and colors.

3 clothing:
somebody dressed
for riding.

4 equipment:
brand-new pieces
of riding gear.

5 mounting/
dismounting:
ladders.

6 teachers: a
teacher you
remember from
school.

7 food: large
buckets of oats or
hay.

8 caring for
hooves:
horseshoe.

9 safe transport:
toy automobiles.

10 competitions:
winners' rosettes.

REMEMBERING TEXT

It's possible to use this technique to memorize a quotation or a passage of text. As an example, imagine you need to remember the words of Charles Sherrington quoted on page 20.

Your first step is to organize the text into its main points:

1   The human brain
2   is an enchanted loom
3   whose millions of flashing shuttles
4   weave a dissolving pattern,
5   always a meaningful pattern,
6   though never an abiding one,
7   a shifting harmony
8   of sub patterns.
9   It is as if the Milky Way
10   entered upon some cosmic dance.

Next, give each of these points a picture clue. Imagine you were illustrating these ideas for a book. What images would you choose?

SHERRINGTON'S VISION
Main Picture: Sherrington's description of the human mind relates a romantic image of the constellations of the Milky Way, full of intricate patterns. These patterns can be effectively channeled to break down information into memorable segments. We all have a rough mental map of our universe and world, so it makes sense to use it as a mental framework to make remembering easier.

THE NEXT STEP IS TO CHOOSE A FRAMEWORK TO HOLD YOUR CHOSEN IMAGES. AS PREVIOUSLY SHOWN, FRAMEWORKS CAN BE MODELED ON ANY LANDSCAPE: BUILDINGS, WALKS, TOWNS—EVEN THE MAP OF THE WORLD. TO USE THE WORLD, HIGHLIGHT TEN COUNTRIES OR CONTINENTS, WORK OUT A ROUTE FROM ONE TO TEN, THEN FILL WITH THE IMAGES.

TIP: TO FURTHER SIMPLIFY THE TEXT, YOU MAY LIKE TO SELECT ONE KEY WORD FROM EACH PHRASE AND USE IT AS A MENTAL LABEL FOR YOUR CHOSEN IMAGE (SEE BELOW).

BRAIN

ABIDING

LOOM

HARMONY

SHUTTLES

SUB PATTERNS

WEAVE

MILKY WAY

MEANINGFUL

COSMIC DANCE

AROUND THE WORLD
Below: The planet earth makes an ideal framework because it is easy to visualize, having been imprinted on our minds since childhood. You can picture it in three dimensions, as a moving globe, or in two dimensions, as a flat picture.

FRAMEWORK C: THE WORLD

1 **GREENLAND**

With a large brain at its center, it sits pulsing on top of the world.

2 **UNITED KINGDOM**

Full of looms, each operated by a cute kitten.

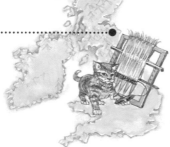

4 **AFRICA**

With the pyramids covered by blankets, their patterns dissolving in the sun.

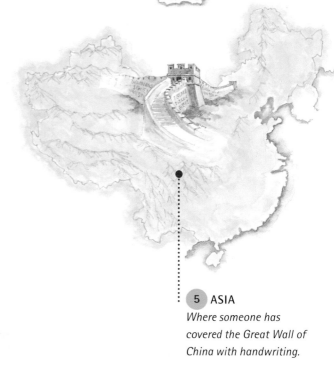

3 **EUROPE**

Where shuttle airplane flights are landing and taking off.

5 **ASIA**

Where someone has covered the Great Wall of China with handwriting.

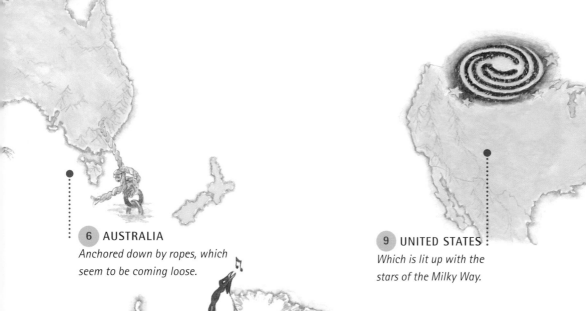

6 AUSTRALIA
Anchored down by ropes, which seem to be coming loose.

9 UNITED STATES
Which is lit up with the stars of the Milky Way.

10 CANADA *Where the sun, moon and stars are dancing together on top of the CN Tower.*

7 ANTARCTICA
Covered with penguins, singing loudly as they waddle about.

8 SOUTH AMERICA
Decorated with complicated patterns and sub patterns.

AROUND THE WORLD

THIS UNUSUAL VERSION OF THE WORLD MAP HAS BEEN DIVIDED INTO TEN AREAS, EACH ONE HOLDING PICTURE CLUES. EACH MEMORABLE IMAGE REMINDS YOU OF A MAIN POINT IN THE ORIGINAL QUOTATION. IF YOU TRAVEL THROUGH THE FRAMEWORK A FEW TIMES, RECALLING WHAT EACH CLUE MEANS, YOU WILL SOON KNOW THE WORDS OF THE QUOTATION BY HEART.

REMEMBERING NUMBERS

BEING ABLE TO REMEMBER NUMBERS IS AN EXTREMELY USEFUL SKILL. NUMBERS ARE EVERYWHERE—PHONE NUMBERS, PIN CODES, PRICES, ADDRESSES, BIRTHDAYS—AND YOU CAN SAVE TIME, IMPROVE YOUR ORGANIZATION SKILLS, AND BOOST YOUR EFFICIENCY BY LEARNING HOW TO COMMIT GROUPS OF NUMBERS TO MEMORY.

Few of us need to remember long sequences of numbers, but we can all benefit from being able to recall a few digits every day. Have you ever stood outside a house trying desperately to remember whether it, or one with a slightly different number, belongs to your friend? Perhaps you know the embarrassment of missing an important birthday, or the inconvenience of forgetting the number of the locker in which you've stored your belongings.

Numbers are only difficult to remember if you try to learn them in their abstract form. Viewed simply as digits on a page, they are intangible and can be confusing. If you change them, you can take control of them in your imagination, making them compatible with the way your mind works.

Without realizing it, you probably do this already with some of the numbers you need to remember. If you notice significant numbers—birthdays, house numbers, anniversaries—within longer sequences, or look for digits making patterns, you are using a natural strategy for boosting your power of recall. Perhaps you choose familiar numbers when you enter the lottery, so that you can remember them from week to week.

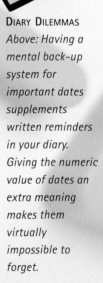

DIARY DILEMMAS
Above: Having a mental back-up system for important dates supplements written reminders in your diary. Giving the numeric value of dates an extra meaning makes them virtually impossible to forget.

A TIME OF GIVING
Above: Birthdays and anniversaries are times of great joy and warmth among family and friends. That is why it is so important to know the days on which they fall.

As soon as a number gains some meaning or identity, suggesting images or feelings, it becomes considerably easier to remember.

In a famous memory experiment carried out in the 1980s, a university student was taught to remember long strings of digits. Initially he had no better than average recall for numbers, but after being taught a specific memory technique, he was able to memorize numbers of eighty digits and more.

His system involved giving numbers meaning. The student, an accomplished athlete, already knew many sports statistics, such as average times in field events. Whenever he saw a string of digits, he looked out for significant numbers within it and compared them with facts already in his memory: When *1217* caught his eye, he thought, "That's an excellent time for the hundred meters." And the digits *236*: "That's almost the same as my personal best for the long-jump."

Suddenly, the numbers became interesting to him, triggering images and emotions. He also found that he could remember them with ease.

You can experiment with this technique yourself, using the following ten-digit number:

6326753660

Ask a friend to read it through a couple of times and try to remember it. Then do the same with a second friend, but this time describe the digits as the score from an exciting tennis match:

6-3 2-6 7-5 3-6 6-0

Get this friend to imagine the match taking place, and to think how each player must have felt after each set.

If you test both friends on their power of recall in a couple of days, you're almost certain to find that the second person remembered more of the number than the first.

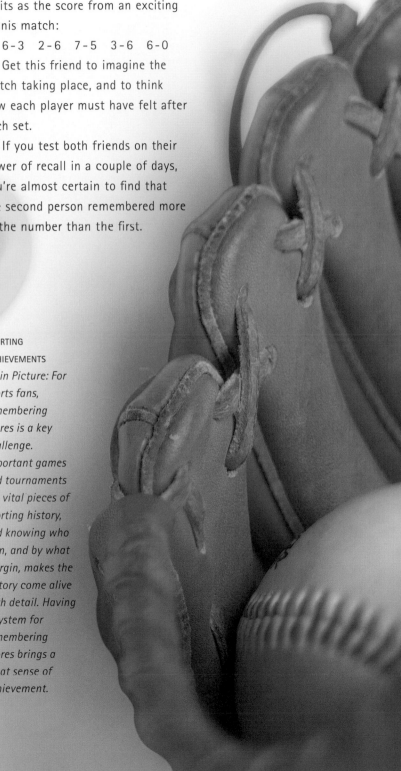

SPORTING
ACHIEVEMENTS
Main Picture: For sports fans, remembering scores is a key challenge. Important games and tournaments are vital pieces of sporting history, and knowing who won, and by what margin, makes the history come alive with detail. Having a system for remembering scores brings a great sense of achievement.

Numbers as Pictures

Using a very simple association technique, you can turn any number into a memorable picture.

Start by assigning an image to each number from 0 to 9, based on the shape of the digit. Later, a range of images can represent each digit, but they will always be based on the following ten ideas:

0 IS A BALL: *Think of this as the healthy, bouncy number, linked with sports and games.*

1 IS A PEN: *It's equipped with a range of colored inks.*

2 IS A DUCK: *This number can fly gracefully, and it is peaceful and serene.*

3 IS AN OPEN PAIR OF HANDCUFFS: *Think of three as a strict disciplinarian, linked with law and order.*

4 IS A SAILING BOAT: *It can float on the water, travelling quickly and smoothly.*

5 IS A HOOK: *Sharply pointed, it is used for lifting and carrying.*

6 IS A CANNON: *This number is powerful, noisy, and violent.*

7 IS A LAMP: *Think of number seven as warm and light.*

8 IS A SNOWMAN: *This is the cold number, linked with wintry weather.*

9 IS AN ICE CREAM CONE: *You can eat this number, and it reminds you of your childhood.*

Spend a few minutes running through these pictures in your mind. Make sure that you can remember the basic image for each of the digits, and try to recapture the qualities associated with all ten numbers—the warmth of seven, for example, or the serenity of two.

To use this system, simply bring to mind the appropriate image for each digit, then connect the images together. It's similar to writing a story—you link the pictures together by creating a memorable chain of events. You might use the first image to do something to the second. You could then put the second image inside the third; the third might transform into the fourth . . . Make the story as vivid as you can and involve all your senses.

Printed at the top of the column on the right are four sets of numbers, four digits in each. To remember the digits 1, 6, 0, and 5, for example, you might imagine using a pen (1) to write on a cannon (6), then loading in a ball (0) and hoisting the whole thing on a large hook (5). Perhaps your pen writes with bright green ink to contrast with the rusty color of the cannon; the ball is a small pool ball; and the hook belongs to Captain Hook, who wants to use this cannon on his pirate ship.

Visualize this scene in your mind's eye, and you'll be able to convert the images back to the original digits.

If you can remember using the pen to write on the cannon, loading in a ball, and hoisting it all on a hook, you're able to recall the numbers 1, 6, 0, and 5.

MEMORABLE PICTURES

Below right: Your imagination allows you to change numbers into memorable pictures, such as the number six into a cannon. As long as you can change them back on demand, it makes sense to store them in this manageable form.

STORY FUN

1605 7324 6582 0935

Dream up a story for each set of numbers, and locate each story within one of your memory frameworks. Choose a framework that you're familiar with, then fix one story in each of the first four locations. Use your imagination fully to visualize the events unfolding in these new surroundings. Perhaps you can make use of furniture or other details already present as the scenery for each story.

If you used Framework B: The Office, you start fixing the numbers 1605 in the first location by picturing an angry office worker (or even yourself!) scrawling (1) graffiti over a cannon (6) because it is blocking the entrance.

For 7324, you might imagine turning on the light (7) in the reception area, only to be clapped in handcuffs (3) by a passing security guard. To escape, you transform yourself into a duck (2) and fly off over the sea, which is dotted with sailing boats (4).

Now finish the story for 1605, and create new ones for 6582 and 0935.

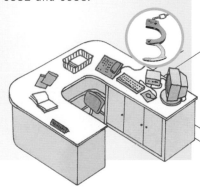

TECHNIQUES AND SKILLS

WITH A LITTLE IMAGINATION, ANY KIND OF INFORMATION CAN BECOME MEMORABLE.

When you use vivid images to represent abstract information, you can place your mental pictures within memory frameworks. These images trigger memories of the original information, and the surrounding framework keeps it all in the correct order, making this strategy particularly useful for learning new skills and procedures.

First, highlight the main elements of the procedure, then categorize and visualize them using the same methods you have used for remembering other lists.

WOODWORKING FOR ALL

The basic technique for cutting a dovetail joint is a perfect example of how skills can be memorized through an initial breakdown, then visualization.

LEARNING A
NEW SKILL
Below left: When learning a new skill, such as woodworking, it is essential that you highlight the key parts of the technique to make sure that you understand it. Understanding is the foundation for remembering. Once you have a list of key parts, assign to each part a memorable image within one of your familiar memory frameworks.

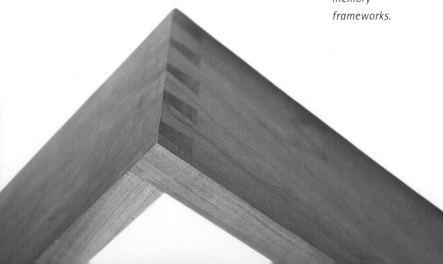

ORGANIZING INFORMATION IS ALWAYS VITAL. IN A LOGICAL ORDER, HERE ARE THE MAIN POINTS OF MAKING A DOVETAIL JOINT.

1 **Preparing:** Prepare the wood and measure out the dovetails.

2 **Selecting:** Select the correct saws, including tenon, coping, and dovetail.

3 **Clamping:** Clamp the pieces to the workbench.

4 **Sawing:** Carefully saw the dovetails.

 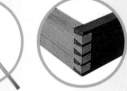

5 **Chiseling:** Use chisels to remove the waste between the dovetails.

6 **Adjusting:** Check the fit of the joint and adjust as necessary.

7 **Finishing:** Gently plane the surface to finish.

1 GREENLAND

A boat has hit an iceberg and the sailors are making dovetail joints to fix rafts together, reminding you to mark out the joints.

4 AUSTRALIA

You might choose Sydney Opera House, which now has a huge dovetail shape sawed out of the roof, as a landmark.

7 ASIA

You focus on the Great Wall of China. Its whole length is now silky smooth, reminding you to plane the joint to finish.

5 ANTARCTICA

Much of the ice has been chiseled away, reminding you to chisel out the waste.

2 UNITED KINGDOM

The people are running around with different saws, reminding you to select your saws.

APPLY TO ANY SKILL

RUN BACK THROUGH THE ROUTE AND YOU'LL FIND ENOUGH PICTURE CLUES AT EACH STAGE TO TRIGGER YOUR MEMORY. APPLY THE SYSTEM TO DOVETAILING OR ANY OTHER SKILL, AND SOON YOU'LL KNOW IT BY HEART. THE PICTURES IN YOUR MIND PROVIDE VIVID REMINDERS OF EACH STEP AND THE SET ROUTE MAKES SURE YOU CARRY THEM OUT IN EXACTLY THE RIGHT ORDER.

6 AFRICA

People are swapping clothes to check the fit. This strange sight will remind you to check the fit of the joint.

3 EUROPE

Trekkers are climbing the Alps, but they have to hold onto trees to keep from falling. This might remind you to clamp the wood to the workbench.

MEMORY EXPANSION

IN ORDER TO EXPAND THE MEMORY, WE MUST NOT BE STIFLED BY
OUR OWN SELF-IMPOSED LIMITATIONS: WE CANNOT GROW UNLESS
WE GO BEYOND OUR IMAGINED CAPABILITIES.

Each framework you create may have a maximum of ten areas, but each area can hold a vast amount of information. If you make each point on your route the starting point for a story, a single framework can have an infinite capacity.

A lack of confidence is usually the biggest obstacle to increasing memory capacity. We become used to feeling uncertain about our ability to learn and remember. Therefore, we set our own limits on what we might be able to achieve and assume that it would be impossible to go beyond them. This belief in self-imposed limits is especially noticeable when there is a large amount of information to learn. A voice in our head tells us that it's simply too much to manage. Not surprisingly, the prophecy comes true.

When you know how to use your memory, the quantity of information turns out to be much less important than it seems. You learn by creating

INFINITE NUMBERS
Below: Memory performers and teachers often demonstrate their ability to remember hundreds of numbers in sequence. It looks impressive, but it's the same basic skill you've already learned. Remove the mental barriers, and the techniques you're perfecting will store just as much as you want.

memorable images and arranging them in connected patterns. If the connections are strong enough, the mental chains should lead you through any amount of information. For example, if you can learn four numbers by constructing a memorable story, there's no reason why you can't carry on the story, going from link to link, and finally memorize 44 or 444 numbers.

PRACTICE MAKES PERFECT
The more you practice, the more confident you'll feel. Resist the temptation to think that the process gets harder as each new piece of information is added. If you keep creating pictures and links, your memory will not let you down.

To prove this to yourself now, try learning a list of fourteen random words. The images and connections have been created for you; simply read them through and picture them in your mind's eye.

This example employs only a small part of one framework—Framework B: The Office, explained fully on pages 60–63. The events in this story unfold in the first three areas, two of which contain five images, the third four.

The words to learn are: businessman, banana, knife, flour, dog, football, cheese, glass, mouse, suitcase, boxer, meat, fishbowl, television.

WHERE DO YOU BEGIN?

Your journey begins at the front door of the building, where a smartly dressed businessman tries to stop you from entering by threatening you with a large inflatable banana. You take out your new knife and burst his banana. It explodes to release a cloud of white flour, which completely covers a passing dog. Picture the poor dog, now covered from head to paw with flour, running blindly into a hedge. You walk into the lobby area, where a game of soccer is taking place. Instead of a ball, the players are using a large piece of cheese. One of them kicks it powerfully and it knocks over a glass, which smashes into hundreds of pieces.

A mouse, which must have been inside the glass, now scuttles to and fro among the chunks and shards strewn over the floor. For safety's sake, you catch the mouse and put it in your suitcase.

The receptionist seems to be absent, and a boxer is working in her place. For a snack, the boxer eats a huge piece of meat, throwing the remains into a fishbowl standing nearby. Unfortunately, the impact knocks over the whole bowl, sending it crashing into an expensive television set.

You now have a carefully connected set of images to help you remember the list. Confidently write them down or read them from memory.

PROGRESS TEST FOUR

FRAMEWORKS IN PRACTICE: IN THIS TEST YOU WILL USE YOUR VISUALIZATION
SKILLS TO PLACE PIECES OF INFORMATION INTO YOUR MEMORY FRAMEWORK.
WORK SLOWLY AND SYSTEMATICALLY WHEN CONSTRUCTING YOUR MENTAL
IMAGES, SO THAT YOU REMEMBER THEM CLEARLY.

MAD ABOUT WOODCARVING

IMAGINE YOU HAVE TO GIVE A TALK ABOUT
WOODCARVING. USE YOUR MENTAL
FRAMEWORK TO MEMORIZE THE MAIN POINTS.

1 History of the hobby

2 Inspiration

3 Equipment and tools

4 Sharpening tools

5 Design

6 Using templates

7 Carving in 3-D

8 Carving in relief

9 Unusual carvings

10 Useful Internet sites

NUMBER SEQUENCE

PRINTED BELOW IS A FIFTEEN-DIGIT NUMBER. SEE HOW QUICKLY YOU CAN
COMMIT IT TO MEMORY USING THE NUMBER SYSTEM EXPLAINED ON PAGES
76–77. CONVERT EACH DIGIT TO AN IMAGE, THEN EITHER CONNECT THE DIGITS
AND PICTURES IN A LINKED STORY OR PLACE THEM IN A MEMORY FRAMEWORK.

3 9 7 1 0 9 8 4 6 3 7 2 3 8 5

*HINT: Once you have successfully remembered the number sequence,
try repeating it backwards. Although this may seem much harder at
first, there's no reason why it should be. Simply follow the chain of
events back to the beginning, or move through your visualized
framework in reverse.*

TECHNICAL SKILLS

PRINTED BELOW IS A TEXTBOOK-STYLE EXPLANATION OF A FLOWER-ARRANGING
TECHNIQUE. BREAK THE INSTRUCTIONS INTO INDIVIDUAL POINTS; DECIDE ON AN
IMAGE TO REPRESENT EACH ONE; THEN FIX THE SEQUENCE AROUND A MEMORY
FRAMEWORK. SEE HOW MUCH OF THE ORIGINAL PROCEDURE YOU CAN RECALL.

"To make a facing arrangement, fill the container with wet
foam. Arrange the leaves in a fan shape at the back of the
container. Cut the stems of the paler flowers short and arrange
them following the shape of the foliage. Add the darker flowers,
arranging them evenly among the paler ones. Insert the delicate
flowers last."

*HINT: Refer to pages 78–79 to remind yourself of the skill-learning
technique.*

RECAP

THE KEY POINT OF THIS CHAPTER IS THAT IMAGES CAN BE CREATED TO REPRESENT ANY KIND OF INFORMATION.

THINK BACK TO THE visualization techniques used in this chapter and imagine yourself as the illustrator of a book or the designer of an advertising campaign. Which would be the most memorable and effective images to represent the materials at hand? Now think of the information you need to remember and transfer it into memorable images.

If you have to learn everything in an article or textbook chapter, pick out the main points and choose an image to represent each point. The images must be able to jog your memory later—think of them as "picture clues" to the original idea—and suited to being slotted into place within memory frameworks. You can use a similar method to remember numbers: think of each number as representing an image, then turn the sequence into a framework containing the images. Do the same thing when memorizing skills and procedures, separating key points and using pictures fixed in memorable patterns to remember the steps in order. Remember that each framework you create can hold vast amounts of information.

BASIC
APPLICATIONS

MANY PEOPLE FORGET INFORMATION BECAUSE FORGETFULNESS HAS BECOME A HABIT. TO START REMEMBERING, YOU NEED TO KICK THE BAD HABIT, AND PUT YOUR POWERFUL MEMORY TO USE IN AS MANY PRACTICAL WAYS AS YOU CAN, FROM NAMES AND ADDRESSES, TO ROAD DIRECTIONS, AND EXAM INFORMATION. THE AMAZING SYSTEMS EXPLAINED IN THIS BOOK WILL REMAIN NO MORE THAN GREAT POSSIBILITIES UNTIL YOU START USING THEM IN REAL WAYS.

COMMON MEMORY NEEDS

PUT YOUR NEW MEMORY SKILLS TO GOOD USE TO
REMEMBER THE PEOPLE YOU MEET, DATES AND
STATISTICS, GENERAL KNOWLEDGE, EXAM
INFORMATION, DIRECTIONS, AND LANGUAGES.
SOON HAVING A GOOD MEMORY WILL BE SECOND
NATURE TO YOU—AND THE ABILITY TO REMEMBER
A WEALTH OF FACTS WILL CHANGE YOUR LIFE.

NAMES AND FACES

WHAT'S IN A NAME?
Above: For many people, knowing a name is not enough to remember it! Your visual memory tells you that you know the face, but retrieving the name is a struggle . . . until you know the steps to success.

Legend has it that Xerxes, the king of Persia, knew every one of his warriors by name. He is said to have had around one hundred thousand men under his command. In modern times, American memory man Harry Lorayne has become famous for memorizing the names of everyone who attends his stage shows. It is estimated that he has memorized more than eight million names.

Think how embarrassing it is when you know the face but cannot recall the name. Now imagine never being in that situation again. There are some basic steps to follow to ensure that you never forget another name, a skill that enhances both your social and professional life.

Many people have problems in this area and find the experience of being unable to summon a name very frustrating. Have you ever been introduced to someone at a meeting or party, then had to introduce them to one of your old friends and found yourself at a loss for either of their names?

It is entirely possible to take control of this area of memory, and reap positive benefits from remembering everyone you meet. Think of how you feel when someone surprises you by recalling your name. It's very flattering to be remembered; it makes you feel important. Learn to recall names yourself, and everyone you meet can become part of your social and professional network.

STEP ONE: DECIDE TO REMEMBER

Rather than assuming you'll forget, make a conscious decision to switch your memory on and to remember new names.

STEP TWO: HEAR THE NAME

When you're being introduced, it's all too easy to put so much effort into smiling, shaking hands, and being witty that you don't listen to the other person's name. If you miss it the first time, you stand no chance of remembering it. So make sure you listen. If possible, use the person's name right away: "Hello Arthur, it's nice to meet you." Be interested in the name, especially if it's unusual. You could ask how it's spelled or what it means. Always concentrate on the name.

STEP THREE: REPEAT THE NAME

During the conversation, drop in the person's name occasionally. At the same time, repeat it to yourself mentally. Can you picture what the name would look like written down? What do you think the person's signature is like?

USING NAMES
Above Right: Try to visualize written signatures to help you remember names. For example, to think of the name Arthur, imagine the legendary King Arthur writing his name in Gothic lettering.
Below: Once you learn distinctive facts about a person, you'll be better able to recall his or her name.

STEP FOUR: CREATE PICTURE CLUES

Create pictures that connect the name with the face. Perhaps the name sounds stately and regal, suggesting a beautiful signature. Or maybe the person is named after a profession and you can use an image of a uniform as a prompt. The person might share a name with an actor who comes to mind. Part of a name might be a word in itself—an object or animal. Try to focus on these images.

STEP FIVE: CONNECT THE PICTURES WITH THE PERSON

Create a link between the person and the images in your mind. People with the names of stars might morph into those celebrities. Or you might picture the person changing color, or making the noise of an animal that will remind you of their name. The next time you meet the person, you'll have powerful picture clues to trigger their name.

"SHE LOOKS LIKE A RABBIT"
Right: If you think that someone resembles a particular animal, make a conscious link between the animal and the person's name.

Arthur, Amy, Brian, Freddie, Elizabeth
Tarquin, Nwanko, Judith, Silvinhao
Eric, Doris, Grizelda, Igor

PUTTING THE THEORY INTO PRACTICE

Here are examples of some images you could use to remember names.

MR. BAKER

If this man was actually a baker, what clues would you be able to see? Perhaps he would be wearing an apron and a hat and holding a large tray of loaves. In your mind's eye, picture him covered with flour and sweating in the heat of the kitchen.

MR. CHURCH

The obvious image here is of a church building. Imagine Mr. Church inside, reading from a large, old-fashioned bible.

MS. FRENCH

What picture clues can you create to suggest that this woman really is French? You could picture her draped in the French flag, eating croissants, or waving to you from the top of the Eiffel Tower.

DR. PRINCE

Maybe you could think of a prince dressed as a doctor, wearing a white coat and a stethoscope over his stately clothes.

MS. BELL

Perhaps you think of Ms. Bell working in a busy office where telephones are constantly ringing.

MR. GOLDBERG

How much of Mr. Goldberg's clothing is gold already? In your imagination, you can make him completely gold.

MISS MARX

This is another famous name. You could picture Miss Marx impersonating the film star Groucho Marx. How would she walk and talk, and how would everyone in the room feel when she started telling jokes?

MRS. MAY

Perhaps you think of "mayday," the international emergency call. Why might Mrs. May be calling for help? You could picture her losing control of her airplane, then calling for help: "Mayday, mayday!"

MR. NICKEL

Images of coins spring to mind, so imagine Mr. Nickel's jacket covered with coins, or picture him wearing flamboyant coin earrings. Perhaps he reaches into his pocket and offers you a large handful of shiny coins.

MRS. PEACE

As the international symbol of peace, you might think of the sound that a dove makes. Where is Mrs. Peace hiding her doves? You could visualize one bursting out of her pocket.

As always, make your images as exaggerated, funny, strange, and vivid as possible. Use them to remember a name a few times, and soon you'll be able to leave the pictures behind and connect the face with the name automatically.

MENTAL FILE CARDS

FOR PEOPLE YOU'RE GOING TO MEET AGAIN REGULARLY, IT IS A GOOD IDEA TO PREPARE A SET OF MENTAL FILE CARDS THAT WILL CONTAIN USEFUL AND INTERESTING FACTS AND DETAILS IN THE MOST EASILY ACCESSIBLE FORM. MENTAL FILE CARDS ALLOW YOU TO SPEAK WITH CONFIDENCE AND TO MAKE THE MOST OF EVERYTHING YOU KNOW ABOUT THE PERSON IN QUESTION.

It is vital to know personal facts about the people with whom you work—their jobs, employers, hobbies, marital status, and so forth. The personal details you remember demonstrate your interest in your colleagues, who are sure to respond positively.

The same holds true for your social contacts. Knowing a few personal details helps you to make interesting conversation and avoid mentioning subjects that may cause offense. Finally, if you remember what people tell you, they're much more likely to remember you.

To start designing your mental file cards, you'll need to expand your number system slightly. So far you have learned images for the digits 0 to 9, but now it's necessary to add on 10, 11, and 12, for remembering birthdays, anniversaries, and appointments.

THE ULTIMATE FILING SYSTEM
Right: Imagine how confident you'd feel if all the information you needed to know about friends, relatives, colleagues, and clients was at your fingertips, just like a set of office file cards.

10: The British Prime Minister lives at Number 10 Downing Street, so the image for this digit is a large, stately door. Words such as formal and solid characterize this number.

11: The image here is a train, because number 11 looks like a pair of railroad tracks. The train is dirty and noisy and it blows out steam and rushes through the countryside.

12: Twelve is the highest number on the clock, so the memorable image here is a watch or clock, ticking away steadily, loudly, and reliably.

Run through these three images in your mind, bringing all your senses into play. Next, check back through the images you learned for the digits 0 to 9, turning back to page 76 if you need to remind yourself what they are.

With this expanded number system, you can add birthdays to names, along with other facts and details about people you're getting to know.

THREE NEW NUMBERS
Left and below: Treat the numbers 10, 11 and 12 as three individual numbers, rather than having to remember 1 and 0, 1 and 1, and 1 and 2. Each has its own key image, and with a little practice you'll be able to call them to mind in an instant. Railroad tracks are an ideal image for the number 11, and also suggest other train ideas for your mental stories.

Mr. Baker's Story

Let's say Mr. Baker was born on February 11. To remember his birthday, you could imagine him trying to squeeze his tray of newly baked loaves onto a train. Every single carriage is full of ducks. They peck at his bread, and he sprinkles flour all over the train as he tries to find a seat.

Seeing Mr. Baker triggers a series of images in your memory. First, picture him dressed as a real baker and carrying a tray of loaves. Next, think of him climbing on board a train full of ducks. The train stands for 11, and the ducks represent the number 2, so Mr. Baker's birthday must be February 11.

Perhaps the train is heading for the countryside, because Mr. Baker is a keen walker. A radio in the carriage could be playing rock and roll to remind you of his favorite sort of music. Use your imagination to build up a scene packed with picture clues, all reminding you of a fact about Mr. Baker. With this information at your fingertips while you're talking, you'll communicate confidently, know the right questions to ask, and come across as very attentive, interested, and organized.

Any type of detail can be given an image, from either the number system or your own imagination, and added to the basic picture you have for everyone you meet.

Visualize Miss Marx telling jokes, using an ice cream cone (9) as a cigar and being handcuffed (3) for disturbing the peace, and you'll remember that her birthday is March 9.

DATES AND STATISTICS

CONNECTED IMAGES

The system you use to remember numbers can be combined with all the other techniques explained so far for easy recall of more complicated dates and statistics.

If you're dealing with lots of numbers, the trick is to use the basic number system with a little more freedom. You already have a special picture image for the numbers 1 through to 12; now you can increase the possibilities dramatically.

Instead of just using the number image to represent each digit, you can pick other connected images. Each basic picture—ball, pen, duck—becomes the heading for a whole group of themed ideas.

Zero is a ball, so it can also be represented by a football player, a golf club, or a bowling alley.

One is a pen, so possible associations include an inkwell, a paintbrush, or an artist.

Here are some suggestions for expanding the rest of the system.

2: The duck: **airplane,** pilot, rocket, sky, space.

3: The handcuffs: policeman, **prison.**

4: The sailboat: sea, **fish,** beach, sailor, surfer.

5: The hook: **coat hanger,** crane, fork, elevator.

6: The cannon: **gun,** bullet, armor, soldier.

7: The lamp: sun, fire, match, **flashlight.**

8: The snowman: snow, rain, ice, **ice-skater.**

9: The ice cream cone: **candy,** lunch, dinner, chef.

10: The door: gate, fence, **furniture,** carpenter.

11: The train: driver, **car,** road, garage.

12: The clock: **watch,** springs, pendulum, diary, calendar.

Spend a minute or so concentrating on each of the numbers, filling your mind with the range of images now open to you for each one. The system works the same way it did before. The only difference is that you choose among a number of pictures to represent each digit.

A REASON FOR THE LINK

With practice, you can turn any digit or group of digits into a memorable picture. The new range of choices also gives you scope to make your images appropriate to the original material. This is essential— you need to build a strong mental link between the imagery you create and your reason for creating it. The images in your mind should automatically prompt you to recall specific facts, just as you should always know how to access the images you need to recapture a particular piece of information.

For example, if you wanted to retain the fact that the United Nations was founded in 1945, you would need to create a link between the imagery you created for the year and the UN itself. You might imagine using a paintbrush (1) to paint the initials "UN" on a lunchbox (9) and then giving it to a naval officer (4) as he walked into the

CONNECTING PICTURES AND PLACES
Left: It's useful to locate your images in an appropriate place, such as a container for pens or paintbrushes, both of which can represent the number 1. The place itself may provide you with some extra details to use in your mental scenario.

elevator (5) at the UN building in New York. That way, you would only have to think of the United Nations to trigger a memory of this scene, and so recall all the information you need: painting a lunchbox and giving it to the naval officer in the elevator reminds you of four digits —1945. The scene in your mind's eye is clearly linked with its subject.

MAKING CONNECTIONS
Below: Allow your imagination to elaborate on the direct connection between numbers and visual images. This way, you'll always have an entertaining way to remember mundane information. The idea of painting "UN" on a lunchbox links the information you wish to remember with the numbers 1 and 9.

EXAMS AND TESTS

LEARN HOW TO PERFORM WELL

BEING ABLE TO PERFORM WELL ON TESTS AND EXAMINATIONS IS CRUCIAL TO REALIZING YOUR AMBITIONS AND DREAMS.

START YOUNG

Below right: It's rare to meet an adult who enjoys taking tests. Young children, on the other hand, can still see them as exciting and fun. Arm your children and grandchildren with the best techniques and always encourage their imagination, and they will keep on enjoying the challenge of testing.

Testing begins early in a child's education, and it becomes increasingly frequent until graduation. Many professions and hobbies also require taking tests from time to time. Job promotions are often tied to exam results, as is the eligibility to participate in some social and recreational activities.

If you are able to review effectively, cope with the rigors of exams, and perform accurately, creatively, and consistently under pressure, you are at a great advantage in many areas of life. So why didn't anyone teach you how? Students are always told what they must know and what will happen if they fail, but they rarely learn how to learn. Most of us grow up feeling afraid of exams and ill-equipped to cope with them.

Approached in the right way, exams can actually be enjoyable. They offer a chance for you to reap the rewards of your work. The process of reviewing the material you have studied can be fun and interesting, and the exam itself can be an exhilarating—not a terrifying—challenge.

The first step is to approach exams in the right frame of mind. How often do people who are about to take exams declare that they're probably going to fail? No wonder pre-test jitters are so common. How can anyone perform while thinking nothing but negative thoughts?

FINDING THE MOTIVATION

To change this pattern of thinking, examine your motivation. Concentrate on the possible rewards of success, rather than on the implications of failure. Perhaps doing well on an exam will get you into a good school, boost your pay-check, gain you a spot in an exciting training program, allow you to try new things, or simply give you a carefree summer. Always bear in mind your reasons for working hard, and concentrate on the benefits the extra effort could bring.

The best way to gain total confidence is to learn your material the right way. Most people go into an exam worried about forgetting, tired from late night crammings, and unsure of what, if anything, they actually know.

Use the best learning strategies, and you can be sure that all the information you need will be at your fingertips, in a form that's easily accessible and useful to you in the exam. Use your trained imagination to visualize yourself remaining calm under pressure, succeeding, and fulfilling your potential.

THE RIGHT ATMOSPHERE

As you study, make sure that you have a suitable environment for learning. The room should be neither too hot nor too cold, and you should sit in a comfortable chair that's not so cozy it will put you to sleep. Shut out distracting noise. Music might help you, but some people require total silence.

Do what you can to keep interruptions to an absolute minimum, and spend a few moments focusing your mind. Perhaps you can return to the relaxation zone you visualized on page 44.

TALK TO YOURSELF

Left and below: You can boost your confidence and sense of well-being by cutting out negative words of self-talk: I hate this, I'm so tired, I'm going to fail . . . Imagine the voice of a coach or motivational speaker, firing you up to feel good and do your best.

A Valuable Investment

Before you start to study, make sure you have all the materials you need—the right notes, textbooks, and journals. Find out exactly what you need to know for this exam, and make sure you understand it. Otherwise your efforts will be pointless. The time you spend preparing to study and review is a valuable investment.

Quality, not Quantity

Carefully organize your time between finding out about and taking the exam. The temptation is to squeeze in as much study time as possible, but it's the quality of your learning that's important. You can tell if your mind is starting to wander. And when it does, stop, take a break, and return when your memory is working again. Study in short bursts, deciding by trial and error which is the best session length for you.

Whatever subject you're learning, the basic memory strategies apply. Break the information into individual points, create memorable images to represent them, then connect the same images to each other in stories or around familiar frameworks.

If you fill each area with images, you can use just a few frameworks to prepare for an entire exam. Names, dates, statistics, and ideas can all be made vividly memorable and fixed into place.

Essential Bits and Pieces
Main Picture: The more organized you are with your study materials, the more organized you'll feel about your exam. Keep a mascot to boost your morale.

For example, you might have divided your modern history review into short sections, then highlighted some of the key facts. In one section, the essential fact could be:

MOUNT EVEREST: FIRST CLIMBED IN 1953 BY HILLARY AND TENSING

In one area in your framework, picture Mount Everest itself. The two climbers could be standing at its base, looking up—Hillary saying he thought it was just a *hill*, while Tensing *tenses* up at the prospect of climbing it.

The climbers use a crane to hoist a police officer into the air to report the weather conditions on the top. The crane represents number 5, and the police officer is 3, reminding you that Everest was conquered in 1953.

The time it takes you to organize your material and to think up appropriate images is time well spent. In the examination itself, all the facts and figures you need are at your fingertips, and you are in a powerfully creative and confident frame of mind.

BRINGING FACTS TO LIFE
Above: As you create your mental pictures, bring in as many real details as you can. For example, if you'd seen photographs of Hillary and Tensing, you could add details of their actual appearance. Bring in your own feelings, too: Imagine how cold it must have been, how the two men might have felt when they reached their goal. You'll find that memory techniques can bring your subject matter to life as well as helping you to remember it.

DIRECTIONS

BECAUSE THE FRAMEWORK SYSTEM IS
BASED ON TAKING MENTAL JOURNEYS, IT'S
AN EXCELLENT STRATEGY FOR LEARNING AND
REMEMBERING DIRECTIONS.

GENDER ISSUES

Research suggests that men and women differ in their
ways of remembering directions. Men tend to rely on
road names and numbers and compass directions, while
women use landmarks and memorable features along the
route. Research also shows, unfortunately, that both men
and women remember directions poorly, getting lost or
forgetting crucial details.

Complicated directions can be difficult to remember
for a number of reasons. They're likely to be given
quickly by someone who doesn't realize how much you
need to know—too much or too little detail can be
confusing. You're likely to be under stress and perhaps
feeling slightly out of control when you ask for
directions, and reluctant to speak up if you'd like to have
them repeated.

The framework system works well because it is based
on a familiar landscape. Directions for a route can be
turned into images and mentally placed, in order, around
your framework. You know the mental journey of your
framework well enough to move around it almost
instinctively to rediscover the carefully ordered memory
clues you've fixed there.

MEMORY MARKERS
*Above left: Road
signs use shape
and color to be
more distinctive
and memorable to
the driver.*

For example, imagine you receive these directions over the phone:

"From your driveway, turn left, then take the first turn on the right. Go to the top of the hill, then turn right and go past the car showroom and the shopping mall, then turn left and pass the airport. Go over the river, and you'll see my house when you take the first driveway on the right."

Next, choose a familiar framework, such as the office, and move through it, placing an image clue corresponding to each point on the route in each framework area. Turn the page to see how this may work.

DIRECTIONS

THE FIRST STEP IS TO BREAK THE INFORMATION INTO SEPARATE POINTS:

turn left

turn right

go to top of hill

turn right

drive past car showroom

drive past the shopping mall

turn left

drive past airport

over the river

turn right

SLOTTING IN THE INFORMATION: FOR THIS DIRECTION
EXERCISE, IF YOU CHOOSE FRAMEWORK B: THE OFFICE,
YOU MIGHT VISUALIZE . . .

4 THE MAILROOM

Only the right half of the mailroom contains letters. All the letters are stamped "important" beckoning you towards them, and, of course, to turn right.

1 THE ENTRANCE . . . .

A large metal stapler is lying on the far left-hand side of the office door, reminding you to turn left as you exit your driveway.

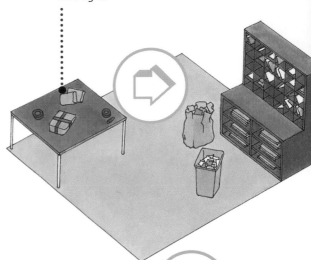

2 THE LOBBY . . . .

The office clock is in the lobby, pushed to the far right of the room, reminding you to turn right.

5 YOUR DESK . . . .

Your work station is covered with toy automobiles, reminding you to go past the car showroom.

3 THE RECEPTION DESK . . . .

The receptionist's switchboard has been placed on top of a large ramp, reminding you to go to the top of the hill.

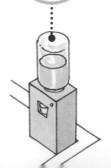

6 THE WATER COOLER

Shopping bags hang on the front of the water cooler, telling you to drive past the shopping mall.

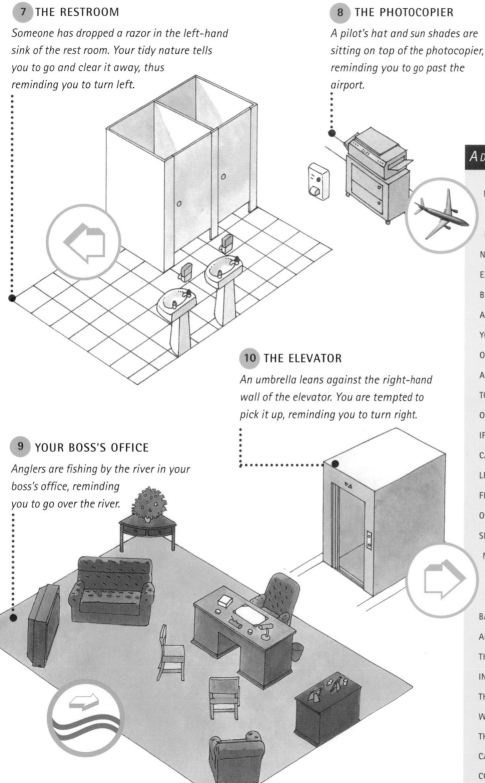

7 THE RESTROOM

Someone has dropped a razor in the left-hand sink of the rest room. Your tidy nature tells you to go and clear it away, thus reminding you to turn left.

8 THE PHOTOCOPIER

A pilot's hat and sun shades are sitting on top of the photocopier, reminding you to go past the airport.

10 THE ELEVATOR

An umbrella leans against the right-hand wall of the elevator. You are tempted to pick it up, reminding you to turn right.

9 YOUR BOSS'S OFFICE

Anglers are fishing by the river in your boss's office, reminding you to go over the river.

ADDING DETAIL

MORE DETAILS CAN EASILY BE ADDED TO THE FRAMEWORK. IF YOU FIND OUT THE NUMBERS OF THE ROADS, FOR EXAMPLE, THEY CAN ALSO BE CONVERTED TO PICTURES AND SLOTTED INTO PLACE. YOU MIGHT PICTURE TWO PAIRS OF HANDCUFFS HANGING FROM A PARTICULAR DOOR HANDLE TO REMEMBER THAT A ROAD ON THE JOURNEY IS ROUTE 33. IF YOU VISUALIZE A LARGE CANNON SITTING AMONG THE LETTERS IN THE MAILROOM, FLICKING THE LIGHT ON AND OFF, YOU REMEMBER THAT THE SECOND TURN IS INTO ROAD NUMBER 67.

PERHAPS YOU WANT TO ADD SOME DISTANCES TO THE BASIC INSTRUCTIONS. THINK ABOUT THE VISUAL CLUES TO THE NUMBERS, THEN INCORPORATE THESE ITEMS INTO THE STORY OF EACH ROOM. WITH THE INSTRUCTIONS IN THIS MEMORABLE FORM, YOU CAN SET OFF FEELING CONFIDENT THAT YOU'LL REACH YOUR DESTINATION.

LANGUAGES

THE MEMORY TECHNIQUES IN THIS BOOK WILL ENABLE YOU TO ORGANIZE AND TRANSFORM INFORMATION TO MAKE IT COMPATIBLE WITH THE MIND'S NATURAL WORKINGS AND THEREFORE EASILY ACCESSIBLE. THIS PROCESS, HOWEVER, STANDS IN STARK CONTRAST WITH TYPICAL LANGUAGE-LEARNING EXPERIENCE.

EASIER THAN YOU THINK
Below: Having some knowledge of foreign languages makes vacations much more enjoyable. Start with a few key words and phrases, understand their origin, and learn how they fit together. Tell yourself there is no such thing as a mental block with foreign languages, and you'll be bilingual sooner than you think.

At school, you probably received no guidance as to how to retain new vocabulary. Even if you passed your exams, you might not have had the confidence to speak the language. You can probably remember some of your foreign language now, but most of it may have left your memory.

In fact, the memory techniques explained in this book are ideal for learning languages. Rather than being a long-winded, frustrating, and seemingly pointless experience, language-learning can be quick, efficient, and rewarding.

START WITH VOCABULARY

The trick to languages is to memorize enough basic vocabulary to use on vacations and business trips, as well as in language classes. At this stage, when you're learning words in a real-life context, your ability to absorb foreign vocabulary increases immeasurably. Unfortunately, most of us fall by the wayside before reaching this point. We assume that language-learning is simply beyond us.

Your imagination holds the key to learning vocabulary. All you need

SANDWICH
Danish: sandwich
Spanish: sandwich
English: sandwich

TENNIS
French: le tennis
German: das Tennis
English: tennis

RADIO
French: le radio
German: das Radio
English: the radio

YOU KNOW MORE THAN YOU THINK
Left: You might be surprised how many words you know, or can guess, in other languages. You already have the foundation for learning a new language, as many languages share the same roots, and are thus easy to relate to each other. These examples show "international" words which are familiar in many languages.

to do is create a picture for each word, with enough detail to tell you everything you need to know.

For every language, choose a mental location for these pictures, perhaps a building that you know.

The first step is to visualize the word in this location. For example, if you were learning a foreign word for tree, you might visualize it in a park; the word for door could be located by a shop door. Give your picture some details to make it memorable.

WORDS THAT STAY THE SAME

Even before you start studying a new language, you already know a surprising amount of vocabulary because many languages are derived from the same ancient language—such as Latin or Gaelic—or from your own mother tongue, such as English. Every time you come across a word that remains unchanged, picture it in your mind's eye, and imagine it becoming transparent. Perhaps it's made of glass and you could be viewing it through an X-ray machine. If you return to your mental storehouse and find one of these transparent images, you'll know that the foreign word is the same as the one you know.

WORDS THAT NEED A HIGHLIGHTING CONNECTION

Some foreign words are just one step away from your own language. If you can work out a link, you can combine it with the original image and leave yourself with a powerful memory clue.

For example, the Spanish word for "finished" is *terminado*—easy to remember if you think of the connecting word "terminated." So you might imagine a "finish" sign hanging in your location, put up by *The Terminator* himself, Arnold Schwarzenegger. Perhaps he crosses out the word "finish" and writes "terminated" instead.

When you think of the word *finished*, you'll remember the word *terminated*, and this will trigger your memory of the Spanish, *terminado*. Always be on the lookout for these connecting words. They provide a bridge between the two languages.

INTERESTING HISTORY

Above: The English word pants and the French word le pantalon *both come from the Italian word* pantalone, *a character in classic Italian comedies.*

WORLDWIDE POPULARITY

Above: Coffee is an international drink and has the same name in numerous languages.

PHYSICAL MEANING

Above: The universal form of sign language, semaphore, is used in many European languages to mean traffic lights.

CREATING WORD CONNECTIONS

If there is no obvious link between words, you need to create one. What does the foreign word sound or look like? The technique is similar to the one for remembering names explained on pages 86–89. Look for associations with the word, or concentrate on the part of it that suggests an image. You then connect that image with the original picture fixed in your location.

For example, the German word for basin is *Becken*. If you are a native English-speaker, you might picture the basin growing a finger and "beckoning" you towards it. Create a memorable connection, and when you think of a basin in future you will see it "beckon" you in your mind's eye, and you will remember the word, *Becken*.

The Spanish word for suitcase is *maleta*. Again, if you are trying to remember the word as an English speaker, you could imagine stuffing mallets into the suitcase. Here are some more links between English and other languages:

FRENCH: the word for door is *porte*, so imagine cutting a porthole in the door.

GERMAN: the word for hat is *Hut*, so you might picture hanging your hat in a special wooden hut.

SPANISH: the word for switch is *interruptor*, so envisage that every time you touch a switch, it interrupts your train of thought.

Some languages have words that require a gender designation. To recall gender, simply add another detail to your visualized picture. You could pick a particular color or smell for all the masculine images, or give all the feminine images a symbol or sound to trigger your memory. Develop your own preferred details, and soon you'll have a mental storehouse full of images that tell you exactly what you need to know about every foreign word.

GENERAL KNOWLEDGE

WHETHER IT'S FOR AN EXAMINATION, A GAMESHOW, PERSONAL INTEREST, IT'S USEFUL TO BE ABLE TO TUR INFORMATION INTO PATTERNS OF MEMORABLE IMAGES. THESE PAGES SHOW YOU HOW.

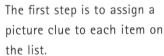

Follow the instructions, and use your imagination to learn the makeup of our solar system.

This example uses Framework A: The House, to remember the planets in order of distance from the sun. The sun is included in the list to emphasize its place at the center of our universe.

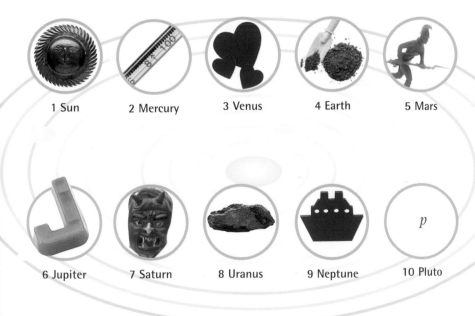

| 1 Sun | 2 Mercury | 3 Venus | 4 Earth | 5 Mars |

| 6 Jupiter | 7 Saturn | 8 Uranus | 9 Neptune | 10 Pluto |

The first step is to assign a picture clue to each item on the list.

1 Sun: the burning sun itself.
2 Mercury: a mercury thermometer.
3 Venus: the goddess of love, perhaps represented by hearts.
4 Earth: a layer of soil.
5 Mars: the god of war; imagine soldiers and battle.
6 Jupiter: the largest planet, so think of a huge letter *J*.
7 Saturn: sounds like Satan.
8 Uranus: glowing uranium.
9 Neptune: the god of the sea; picture ships on the ocean.
10 Pluto: the smallest planet; visualize a tiny letter *p*.

Next, visualize each image in place within the framework:

1 THE FRONT DOOR

Picture the Sun shining onto the front door, warming up the shiny door knocker.

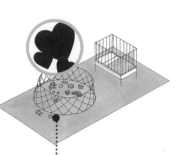

3 THE NURSERY

The nursery is covered with romantic paper hearts, left there by Venus.

7 THE DINING ROOM

Satan (sounding like Saturn) has stuck his hot pitchfork into the antique dining room table, charring the wood surface.

8 THE KITCHEN

Radioactive uranium (sounding like Uranus) has been discovered under the kitchen sink.

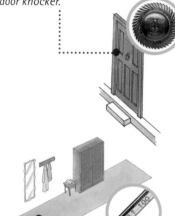

2 THE HALLWAY

A huge Mercury thermometer is placed on the hallway wall to show the room temperature.

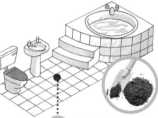

4 THE BATHROOM

A layer of muddy earth has been spread across the bathroom floor, ruining the preparations for your big night out.

9 THE STUDY

Water pipes have burst under the study floor, which is now under water, much to the delight of Neptune.

5 THE BEDROOM

All across the bedroom, a huge battle is being fought, watched over by the warlike Mars.

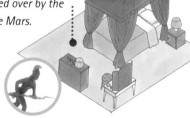

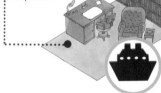

KEEP PRACTICING

RUN BACK THROUGH THE FRAMEWORK IN YOUR MIND AND PRACTICE RETRIEVING ALL THE PICTURE CLUES, AND SOON YOU WILL KNOW THIS INFORMATION BY HEART.

6 THE LIVING ROOM

A huge letter J has crashed through the roof of the living room, dropped by Jupiter.

10 THE SUNROOM

One of the sunroom plant pots contains a tiny letter p—Pluto.

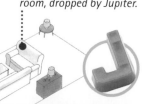

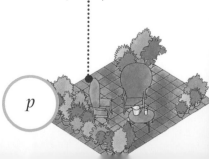

p

PROGRESS TEST FIVE

WHO'S THAT?

YOUR CHALLENGE IS TO COMMIT THE FOLLOWING PEOPLE TO MEMORY:

JOHN TAYLOR	MARY MANCINI	TOM D'ANGELO	LILY CHUNG	CARL OAKLEY
A musician who enjoys playing hockey.	A nanny who owns two dogs and loves shopping for clothes.	A traveling salesman with a wife named Jill.	An artist and keen Internet user.	A designer who takes vacations in Florida.

TRY TO REMEMBER AS MUCH AS POSSIBLE ABOUT THE FIVE PEOPLE. TURN THE PAGE TO TEST YOURSELF.

WHICH WAY NOW?

CHOOSE A MEMORY FRAMEWORK TO LEARN THE FOLLOWING SET OF DIRECTIONS. AS SOON AS YOU FEEL CONFIDENT THAT YOU KNOW IT ALL, TURN THE PAGE TO TEST YOURSELF.

"Leave the parking lot by the north gate and turn left onto route 25. Continue as far as the church. Turn left, and drive four miles. At the crossroads, turn left, then right, and I'll meet you by the gas station."

LEADING MEN

HERE IS A LIST OF THE PRESIDENTS OF THE UNITED STATES SINCE WORLD WAR II. CHOOSE A FAMILIAR FRAMEWORK, CREATE A PICTURE CLUE FOR EACH OF THE NAMES, THEN FIX THEM ALL IN PLACE IN THE MOST MEMORABLE WAYS YOU CAN THINK OF.

Truman	Ford
Eisenhower	Carter
Kennedy	Reagan
Johnson	Bush
Nixon	Clinton

HOW WELL DID YOU DO?

WHO'S THAT?

1   2   3   4   5

....

....

WHICH WAY NOW?

SEE IF YOU CAN RECITE OR WRITE DOWN THE SET OF
DIRECTIONS. USE MENTAL TRIGGERS TO HELP YOU REMEMBER.

....

....

....

....

....

....

....

LEADING MEN

USING YOUR MENTAL FRAMEWORK, RECITE THE NAMES OF
THE PRESIDENTS IN THE CORRECT ORDER.

....

....

....

....

....

RECAP

BEING ABLE TO PUT A NAME TO A FACE IS A VITAL
SKILL IN SOCIAL AND BUSINESS LIFE. TO AVOID THE
EMBARRASSMENT OF FORGETTING WHO'S WHO,
CAPITALIZE ON AN IMPRESSIVE USE OF MEMORY.

FOLLOW THESE STEPS when improving your
memory in social situations. Any information can be made
compatible with the way your memory works.

- Remember a person's name by bringing to mind an image
  that the name suggests, exaggerating the picture, or
  creating some other link, and connecting the imagery
  with the person.

- Create "mental file cards" that use number imagery to
  note important dates such as birthdays and anniversaries.
  Any information can be turned into a simple list and
  learned by using well-thought-out imagery.

- Use your imagination to absorb a new language, by
  highlighting similarities between foreign words and their
  definitions. If there appears to be no connection between
  words, create one: Pick something the word sounds like
  and connect that with its real meaning.

ADVANCED APPLICATIONS

MEMORY TECHNIQUES CAN BE USED IN ANY AREA OF LIFE. WITH YOUR NEWLY ACQUIRED MEMORY FRAMEWORKS, BASED ON REAL OR FANTASY LOCATIONS, YOU CAN MENTALLY REHEARSE EVERY NEW CHALLENGE, THEN MEET IT WITH STRENGTH AND CONFIDENCE WHEN IT ARISES. YOU CAN EVEN CREATE "VIRTUAL PRACTICE ZONES" WHERE YOU REHEARSE YOUR SUCCESS UNTIL THE ONLY PICTURES AND EMOTIONS LEFT IN YOUR MIND ARE POSITIVE AND INSPIRATIONAL ONES.

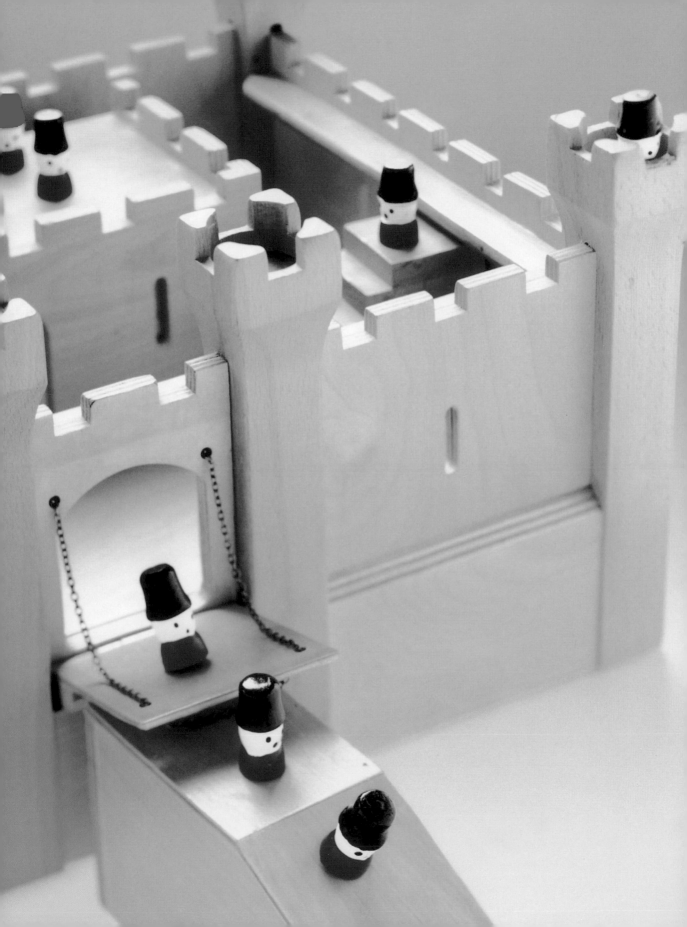

GOOD ORGANIZATION

AS WE'VE SHOWN, THE MEMORY STRATEGIES OUTLINED IN THIS BOOK CAN BE APPLIED TO ANY MENTAL CHALLENGE. THIS CHAPTER DEMONSTRATES SOME EVEN MORE SPECIFIC MEMORY TECHNIQUES. IT ALSO HIGHLIGHTS SOME OF THE LESS OBVIOUS WAYS IN WHICH A POWERFUL MEMORY CAN HELP YOU.

Central to every good memory technique is good organization. Information is sorted, simplified, then rearranged into manageable patterns. By practicing this type of thinking, you'll be more capable of prioritizing information and you'll approach every challenging situation in a calm way.

You can, for example, take all the stress out of preparing to go on vacation. Memory strategies will help you plan the tasks you have to complete before leaving, remember exactly what to take with you to the airport, and keep track of flight details and hotel information. Later, at the end of the vacation, you can ensure that you and your belongings return home safely.

CREATING EFFECTIVE SYSTEMS

Practice putting your skills into action with this list of vacation tasks.

BEFORE LEAVING:
Cancel papers; tell neighbors; take dog to kennel.

THINGS TO BUY:
Sunscreen; insect repellent; film.

ITEMS TO PACK IN CARRY-ON LUGGAGE:
Passports; tickets; money; camera.

SPECIAL ITEMS FOR SUITCASE:
Sunscreen; insect repellent; guidebooks; bathing suit.

FLIGHT DETAILS:
Outgoing: Pan Am flight 219, due to leave at 2:30 p.m.

Return: Pan Am flight 220, returning at 10:45 a.m.

HOTEL INFORMATION:
The Palms, Ocean Drive.

EXTRA DETAILS

It makes sense to organize this information so you leave mental space for a few more details:

Parking space at airport.

Hotel room number.

Combination for safe in hotel room.

To do this, you would leave some areas of your chosen memory framework empty, ready to fill with image clues once the information is available.

CREATING SYSTEMS
Right and Far Left: You need to have both organizational and creative skills to implement and manage effective memory systems. Such skills can be used to great effect when planning a summer vacation.

FRAMEWORK D: THE CASTLE

ON THE NEXT TWO PAGES, A FURTHER MEMORY FRAMEWORK SHOWS HOW YOU CAN MEMORIZE THE TRAVEL LIST QUICKLY AND PRACTICALLY. FRAMEWORK D: THE CASTLE, IS MADE UP OF THE FOLLOWING TEN KEY AREAS, BASED ON AN IMAGINATIVE FANTASY LOCATION.

10 THE STABLES ....
Horses and donkeys are fed and groomed in these old stone buildings. Sometimes, they are taken out of the castle confines to graze in the surrounding fields.

1 THE PATH TO THE CASTLE
What details can we imagine here? The dusty path, well trodden by horses, carts, soldiers, and traders.

2 THE GATE AND DRAWBRIDGE
This imposing entrance to the castle will be a hive of activity. Public notices may be pasted by the gate and the drawbridge will be taken up and down on command. ....

3 THE MOAT ....
The moat acts as a defensive barrier outside the castle walls. It may contain a few ducks and fish, plus various objects which have fallen into the water.

4 THE LOOKOUT TOWER ....
Day and night, this is where the castle soldiers keep a lookout for attacking armies.

9 THE HIGH TOWER
The highest tower in the kingdom, this vantage point displays a bright heraldic flag.

VISUALIZE THE AREAS

AS ALWAYS, SPEND A FEW MINUTES STUDYING THE FRAMEWORK AND VISUALIZING THE AREAS WITHIN IT IN YOUR MIND. PRACTICE TAKING A MENTAL WALK FROM THE PATH TO THE TOWER AND BACK AGAIN, ADDING A FEW DETAILS OF YOUR CHOICE TO EACH OF THE TEN AREAS IN TURN.

8 THE COURT BALCONY
Royalty and other nobility regularly appear on this balcony to greet their loyal subjects.

7 THE FANFARE TURRET
Great announcements are made from this turret, accompanied by a lively fanfare played by the court musicians.

6 THE DEFENSIVE WALLS
The defensive walls are very tall and virtually indestructible. Occasionally castle inhabitants compete to climb up and down the wall on a rope.

5 THE MARKET STALLS
A range of everyday activities takes place here. All sorts of goods are bought by the castle inhabitants; these are sold by lively stall-holders who loudly advertise their wares.

SLOTTING IN THE INFORMATION: PRACTICE USING THIS ROUTE TO ORGANIZE YOUR VACATION, FILLING EACH AREA WITH MEMORABLE, ORGANIZED PICTURE CLUES. FOR EXAMPLE, PUT REMINDERS OF THINGS TO BUY BEFORE YOUR TRIP IN ONE AREA, AND REMINDERS OF HOTEL INFORMATION IN ANOTHER.

1 THE PATH TO THE CASTLE

Before Leaving: By the path stands a large bulletin board covered with job postings. An old newspaper is blowing in the doorway. You notice that there is a picture of your neighbor on the front page. He's been charged with stealing your dog.

2 THE GATE AND DRAWBRIDGE

Things to Buy: Rows of shopping bags are lined up on the drawbridge. As you walk towards them, you realize that someone has smeared the planks on the bridge with slippery sunscreen, which is attracting a swarm of biting insects. You swat them with your photographic film.

3 THE MOAT

Items to Pack for Carry-on: An old sign floats in the moat and painted on it is a piece of carry-on luggage. By the side of the moat is a self-service passport booth. You go to the booth to have your pictures taken, but airplane tickets pop out of the machine instead. You beat your fists against the machine in frustration. A reporter rushes up and photographs the event.

4 THE LOOKOUT TOWER

Special Items for Suitcase: You look out from the tower and see your luggage scattered around the castle. You run down and open one of the bags and find it full of leaking sunscreen. The same swarm of insects gather around the sticky mess. This time you use your guidebooks to swat them. Then, to make sure you are free of them, you put on your bathing suit and dive into the moat for a swim.

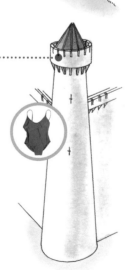

5 THE MARKET STALLS

Outgoing Flight: An airplane has landed on the market stalls. Ducks (2) gather round to watch, and one starts painting (1) an ice cream cone (9). The paint drips onto one of the other ducks (2), who calls two police officers (3), who have been playing volleyball (0) with the airplane passengers.

8 THE COURT BALCONY

Hotel Information:
The servants decide to liven up the court balcony with tropical palm trees and an ocean mural hung over the side.

10 THE STABLES

Safe Combination: If you use the safe in your room, you can use the stables to store the number images for the combination.

6 THE DEFENSIVE WALLS

Return Flight: The pilot (2) and copilot (2) climb the walls to call for help. They kill time by playing baseball (0), then write (1) an SOS on the ball (0). They throw it into the moat and it catches on a fishing hook (5).

9 THE HIGH TOWER

Room Number:
The high tower is empty, ready for you to add picture clues when you know your room number.

A RELIABLE BACK-UP

FILLED WITH IMAGES AND MEMORABLE STORIES, THIS VERSATILE FRAMEWORK ALLOWS YOU TO CONTROL ALL THE PLANNING OF YOUR VACATION— AND GIVES YOU SCOPE TO ADD MORE INFORMATION AS YOU GET IT. YOU'LL FEEL ORGANIZED AND CONFIDENT FROM THE MOMENT YOU CANCEL THE NEWSPAPERS TO THE SECOND YOU GET BACK HOME.

7 THE FANFARE TURRET

Parking Details: The fanfare turret is empty for now. You can use this area to announce the images that remind you where you parked your automobile.

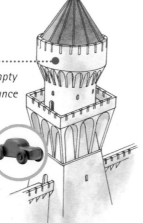

SPEAKING FROM MEMORY

RESEARCHERS SUPPOSEDLY DISCOVERED THAT THE MAJORITY OF US FEAR PUBLIC SPEAKING MORE THAN WE FEAR DYING. AT A TYPICAL FUNERAL, THEN, MOST PEOPLE WOULD RATHER BE LYING IN THE COFFIN THAN GIVING THE EULOGY.

IN THE LIMELIGHT
Main Picture: Don't worry if your head is full of negative mental pictures about public speaking. You can use your imagination to re-draw the experience in a more positive light.

Why do we have such a dread of speaking to an audience? It can hardly be that we're unsure of what we're talking about, because most of us are called upon only to talk about subjects we know well. Even when preparation and research are involved, it isn't the work beforehand that inspires terror, it's the performance itself—specifically, remembering what to say under pressure.

We're afraid of having our minds go completely blank in front of an audience. We fear being questioned and forgetting all the answers. We fear what people will think if we show we're nervous and out of control. And of course, the more nervous we are, the more our memories flatten. Most people would do anything to get out of giving a speech. So what about the few who seem to have no fear, whose memories are strong under pressure? We can all name people who seem to thrive in the spotlight, giving entertaining talks, presentations, and interviews from memory. They have a skill that is built upon a number of key factors:

1 EYE CONTACT

A speaker who reads from notes, looking down all the time, never engages the audience eye to eye. As a result, it appears that they have done a poor job of preparing, which is often far from the truth. They are probably also getting more and more nervous by avoiding looking at the audience and not knowing how they are reacting. Such a speaker stands very little chance of becoming comfortable with the listeners or making a positive impression.

2 UNDERSTANDING

When you read from notes, it's all too easy to let your mind wander. When speaking from memory, on the other hand, you're using imagery to remind yourself of the main points, so you're constantly thinking about the meaning and significance of each part of your talk. Creating the mental journey allows you to focus your thoughts, and you come across as a well-prepared and knowledgeable speaker.

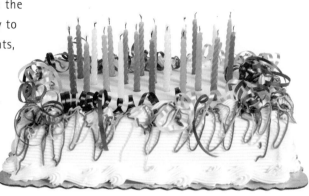

3 ALTERATIONS

When you use the imagery techniques in this book to speak from memory, what you say is not fixed rigidly. You know all the key points in their proper order, but you also have the power to change whatever you want. Add new details, absorb suggestions from the audience, even alter the sequence of your ideas so that you can update your presentations and keep them fresh.

4 TIME MANAGEMENT

When you're using a memory framework to deliver your presentation, you have a good sense of how far through the talk you are at any given time. You can choose to speed up or slow down to suit particular time constraints, always being sure to finish at the right moment, having said everything as planned.

5 CONFIDENCE

With a strong memory, you don't need to fumble with notes or cue cards. You can be confident that all the information you need is at your fingertips. You can therefore talk fluently and knowledgeably, impress people with your obvious interest and intelligence, and handle any number of surprise questions, comments, or challenges.

PARTY CELEBRATIONS
Above: Birthdays and anniversaries are a time when you may be asked to give speeches and announcements. Strong memory skills will inspire you with confidence instead of terror.

DELIVERING A SPEECH FROM MEMORY

THERE ARE JUST FIVE STEPS TO FOLLOW TO
PREPARE AND DELIVER A SPEECH FROM MEMORY:

STEP ONE

Decide what you want to say. Jot down some general points, then add more detail. Play around with the structure until it's clear and organized.

STEP TWO

Pick out the key points. Highlight the main areas of your presentation. Divide it into chapters or sections like a book.

STEP THREE

Design picture clues. You need to choose an image to represent each area of your talk. In a book, how might each point be illustrated? Make each image as memorable as possible.

STEP FOUR

Decorate your memory framework. It is particularly important to choose one you're comfortable with, as you will visualize it automatically when you're speaking from memory, moving instinctively from one area to the next as you progress. Once you've decided on the framework, fix a key image into each of the areas. You're dedicating each area to a particular subject within your talk.

STEP FIVE

Add more detail. Once you've got the basic framework of images in place, you can add extra picture clues. Some areas will need no more than the key images, but others will require lots of additional picture clues to remind you of numbers, names, facts, and dates.

YOU'RE A STAR
Main Picture: Although not everyone gets the opportunity to receive an Oscar, most people will, at some time, need to deliver a speech from memory. Whatever the event, the five-step preparation plan will enable you to enjoy the occasion and feel a sense of achievement.

OFFICE CHALLENGE

For instance, a company manager might have to give a presentation outlining the current state of the business, along with plans for the future. In laying out the talk, the manager's first few ideas might include: finances, training, incentives, and targets.

The image for **FINANCES** could be a pile of money bags, filling up the first area in a memory framework.

The furniture in the second area might be covered with stop watches and sports equipment, symbolizing **TRAINING**.

For **INCENTIVES** the image could be a chunky bar of chocolate candy.

TARGETS could be shooting gallery targets, or a dart board.

Say the key figure in the section on finances is 1.3 million. As a visual link to this number, the manager could imagine painting (1) some handcuffs (3) on a wall within the first area of the framework. Every area within the framework could be decorated in this way—a basic image surrounded by reminders of connected details.

Get used to speaking from memory, and your skills as a communicator will improve immeasurably. You'll have the information you need to present talks, lead meetings, or give interviews wherever you happen to be and however short the notice you're given. In time, you'll learn to relish every opportunity you get to demonstrate your mental strength.

ADAPTING NUMBER IMAGES
Right: Adapting number images is a key skill for remembering figures. The concept of painting is ideal for the number one, as it is such a visual reference to the number.

TOTAL PREPARATION

BESIDES MEMORIZING ALL THE IMPORTANT INFORMATION, YOU ALSO
NEED TO USE YOUR IMAGINATION TO GET IN THE RIGHT FRAME OF
MIND TO SUCCEED IN MEETING ANY CHALLENGE. YOU CAN USE
MENTAL IMAGERY TO RELAX, FOCUS ON THE CURRENT TASK, AND
REHEARSE KEY ELEMENTS BEFORE TACKLING THEM FOR REAL.

KEY FACTS
*Above and Below: Highlighting
details, such as dates and times,
in advance prepares all the
information you need before your
intellectual challenge, whether it
is a television sports quiz or other
general knowledge test.*

Imagine you have been chosen to be a contestant
on a television quiz show. You might have the
following practical facts to remember:

1 Date of recording: February 12th
2 Time to be at the studios: 4 p.m.
3 Address of the studios: Rose Street
4 Name of the researcher meeting you: Richard Martini

You would need to know the topics for each round:

5 Round One: General knowledge
6 Round Two: First specialized subject (baseball)
7 Round Three: Specialized subject (movie history)

You might also be thinking about your performance on
television, with a focus on remembering to:

8 Speak clearly, slowly, and confidently

All this information can be assigned picture clues and slotted into place in a mental framework. Two extra, specially designed areas would make that framework particularly useful—one zone to remind you of your motivation for taking part, and another zone to help you relax and focus your mind.

THE MOTIVATION ZONE

The motivation zone could be filled with imagery of the prizes at stake to remind you why you're putting in such effort. This room might also contain images conveying the other benefits of a good performance, including your family's pride, your friends' awe, and your own sense of accomplishment.

THE RELAXATION ZONE

The relaxation zone should be a version of the place you chose on page 43 to help you calm yourself and focus your thinking. Locating it within this framework would give you a valuable resource alongside the stores of factual information.

Using Framework A: The House (see pages 56–57), the following pages demonstrate how a single framework can be adapted to help you prepare for all the different elements of a challenge.

RUBIK'S CUBE
Main Picture: The Rubik's Cube took the world by storm as a new and exciting puzzle. Those who solved the conundrum—often children competing against the clock—utilized the colors, squares, and planes of the cube to construct and remember the required movements.

AT HOME IN THE TV STUDIO

FRAMEWORK A: THE HOUSE, IS USED HERE TO
REMEMBER THE PRACTICAL INFORMATION, TOPIC
LISTING, AND PERFORMANCE REQUIREMENTS FOR
THE QUIZ EXPLAINED ON PAGE 122.

1 THE FRONT DOOR

*You might convert the date—
2/12—into a duck (2) busily writing
(1) next to another duck (2), as
both birds sit on the doorstep. The
first duck is writing in his diary to
remind you that the images here
represent a date.*

4 THE DINING ROOM

*A researcher is sitting at the table—you're
amazed to see that it's Richard Gere,
holding a cocktail.*

5 THE KITCHEN

*Encyclopedias and general knowledge
books are stored throughout the kitchen—
in the oven, the sink, and even slotted into
the toaster.*

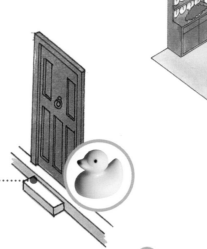

2 THE HALLWAY

*For four o'clock, picture a huge boat (4)
blocking your path. There's a clockface
design on the sail, reminding you that the
image here represents a time.*

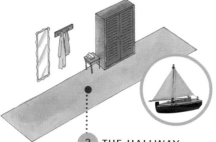

3 THE LIVING ROOM

*This room is full of roses. There's a
picture on the wall of the studio you'll
be visiting, and the roses are growing
around it. Remember these picture to
think of Rose Street, the address.*

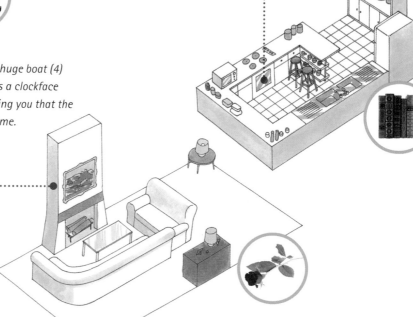

10 THE NURSERY

This is your place to unwind, so paint the walls your favorite colors, set up the most comfortable chair, and adjust the lighting for maximum relaxation. When you enter this room, leave all negative feelings behind and achieve a state of focus and calm.

8 THE BEDROOM

You might picture yourself sitting up in bed, practicing your performance. You use props to help you, picking up a microphone to make sure you speak clearly, using a metronome to help yourself speak slowly, and leafing through a self-help book to boost your confidence.

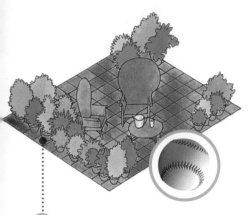

6 THE SUNROOM

A full-scale game of baseball has started here. Picture some of the game's legends negotiating the wicker chairs, and having to squint in the bright sunlight.

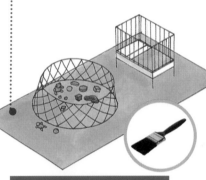

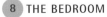

REHEARSE THE ROUTE

BEFORE THE CHALLENGE ITSELF, USE THIS FRAMEWORK TO REHEARSE ARRIVING ON TIME, COMPLETING EACH OF THE ROUNDS, PERFORMING TO THE BEST OF YOUR ABILITY, STAYING MOTIVATED, AND KEEPING CALM. A MENTAL VISIT TO EACH OF THE ROOMS IN TURN WILL PROVIDE YOU WITH POWERFUL PICTURE CLUES FOR EVERYTHING YOU NEED TO REMEMBER AND WILL INFUSE YOU WITH BOTH MOTIVATION AND CALM. DURING THE PROGRAM ITSELF, MAKE RETURN VISITS IN YOUR MIND TO REMAIN FULLY IN CONTROL OF AN OTHERWISE PRESSURIZED SITUATION.

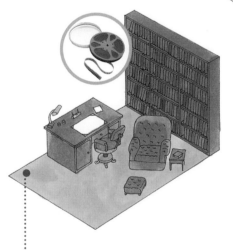

9 THE BATHROOM

This is your motivation zone, and the room is packed with prizes including money, electronics, vacation tickets, and trophies. On the wall, there is a photograph of you winning an Oscar as proud friends and family look on. Every time you visit this room, your motivation receives a powerful boost.

7 THE STUDY

This room is full of movie legends. Marilyn Monroe is sitting at the desk, typing. Harrison Ford as Indiana Jones is swinging from the lights. Arnold Schwarzenegger is searching through the books for his favorite action-packed novel.

MEMORY AND SPORTS

LEARN TO BE A WINNER WHATEVER THE COMPETITION OR SPORT.

All top athletes know that winning is both a physical and a mental achievement. They train their minds to give them an edge over their competition. Sports enthusiasts at any level can reap the rewards of a powerful mind.

Mental checklists can help you to pick up a particular skill or to hone a technique. Use your memory power to learn points from a checklist and let these points instruct you every time you practice. Soon the skill itself will become natural and instinctive.

PRACTICE MAKES PERMANENT
Main Picture: Use your imagination to practice only the right moves of your chosen sport and to eliminate the bad habits. Some sports teams train to the taped chants of opposition supporters to help the players get used to the conditions they'll face. Whether the sport is golf or tennis, being prepared for the conditions in which you'll play is the first step to conquering the various challenges of the competitive environment.

THE GOLF LESSON

A golfing beginner might receive the following pre-swing checklist:

1 Choice of club

2 Grip

3 Foot position

4 Teeing off

5 Timing

6 Height of backswing

7 Downswing

8 Follow through

The student golfer could easily give each of these ideas a picture clue, locating the images within a chosen memory framework.

There might be a huge golf club in the first room or area; something gripping his or her hand in the second; footprints in the third; a model drinking tea in the fourth . . . and so on. By mentally moving through this framework, the golfer would have reminders for every item to check, and the routine would soon become instinctive. A memory system like this simply speeds up the learning process, and ensures that the habits you pick up are the right ones.

VISUALIZING SUCCESS

It's also important to use your imagination to visualize success. A coach once accused the great Olympic runner Jim Thorpe of skipping training. He'd been spotted reclining in a chair, feet up and eyes closed, while the rest of his team slogged it out on the track.

"Why aren't you training?" the coach demanded.

"I am," replied Thorpe. He had been winning races in his mind, checking every possible detail of his technique, imagining the perfect performance, and building it up into a "memory" that he could refer to later. He was designing mental images to help crystallize the key points of technique and strategy, as well as the motivating thoughts that would give him the edge in the heat of competition.

> **66** *You must feel at home anyplace you play.* **99**
>
> Lee Trevino
> Golfer

KNOW YOUR GOLF COURSE
Below: Golf courses are notoriously varied in the way they challenge the player. If you can imagine a course's hurdles prior to playing, you will play a better game that day.

FEELING AT HOME

Your imagination lets you go anywhere, giving you an invaluable capacity for acclimatizing yourself before a sporting event. After winning Wimbledon in 1977, British tennis player Virginia Wade explained how she'd visited Center Court in her mind on the morning of the final. Golfer Lee Trevino has said, "You must feel at home anyplace you play," indicating that you must feel at peace with your environment, whatever the conditions. Your imagination allows you visit anywhere in advance—a football field, golf course, or riding

track—so you can arrive at the real location with feelings of familiarity.

It is important to develop habits that help rather than hinder. For the next ten seconds, DO NOT think about elephants. Now, of course, it's impossible not to. In the same way, many athletes find that uncontrolled thoughts are among their biggest problems. Preparing for a vital putt, all they can think of is the ball missing the hole; or during a long tennis rally, they keep imagining their next shot as a mishit. Mental rehearsal can help avoid this pitfall. If you only visualize successful results, positive thoughts will come more naturally than negative ones.

MENTALLY PREPARED

Mental exercises can help you create a zone of absolute relaxation and perfect concentration for your pre-game mental rehearsal. Having practiced in advance, you will find it easier to achieve this state during real play. This is how golfer Arnold Palmer describes it: "You're involved in the action and vaguely aware of it, but your focus is not on the commotion but on the opportunity ahead. I'd liken it to a sense of reverie . . . the insulated state a great musician achieves in a great performance . . . not just mechanical, not only spiritual; something of both, on a different plane and a more remote one."

Another of the game's greats, Jack Nicklaus, describes watching himself on a kind of mental movie screen, zooming in to see details of the perfect technique. He has said that his game is ten percent about actual swing while 40 percent is setup—his version of the checklist on page 126—and 50 percent is mental rehearsal.

Athletes are good at remembering what it feels like to lose, as well as to win. British sprint star Linford Christie says powerful memories of failure fuel his desire for victory. You can learn from failure not by dreading its recurrence, but by creating picture

ONE RACE, A THOUSAND PRACTICE RUNS
Left: Top athletes imagine running their perfect race countless times before the event. As a result, they "instinctively" know what to do when race day comes.

clues for the things that went wrong so that you can avoid them in the future. One useful technique: Visualize the moment of failure in as much detail as possible. Then mentally alter each piece of the picture until the outcome can only be unqualified success. That way, you'll have strong memories of successful techniques, as well as the confidence that you can control your thoughts during competition.

> **❝**I imagine watching myself on a mental movie screen, zooming in to see details of the perfect technique.**❞**
>
> Jack Nicklaus
>
> Golfer

PLAYING CARDS

THE ABILITY TO REMEMBER SEQUENCES OF PLAYING
CARDS IS AMONG THE MOST IMPRESSIVE
APPLICATIONS OF A POWERFUL MEMORY. IF YOU
CAN MEMORIZE AN ENTIRE DECK OF CARDS, YOU'LL
PROBABLY REMEMBER JUST ABOUT ANYTHING.

Memory can also help you win card games, even if you only need to remember a few cards at a time. In addition, using your memory to enhance card playing will boost your observation skills, increase your speed of thought, and give you an enormous sense of confidence.

To remember playing cards, you need to invest a little time in learning a specific system. As with numbers, decide on a key image to represent each of the 52 cards—then use those images to form scenes and stories and to fill memory frameworks.

Learning 52 images may seem like a daunting task, but there's a clear pattern to the system, based on the technique for numbers explained on pages 74–77. Once you've learned the images and started to use them, it won't be long before you can instantly recall the picture for each card, and vice versa. In this way, a card's suit gives you a general guide to the sort of image used to represent it. The specific image is governed by the meaning of the card number taken from the system explained earlier on page 76.

CARD CONFIDENCE
Below: Learning to remember all 52 cards boosts your playing confidence tremendously, as well as your observation skills and concentration span.

- All the heart cards have images connected with love, care, and the human body.

- The diamonds are connected with riches, jewelry, and craftsmanship.

- The images for the clubs are linked with crime, weaponry and violence.

- The pictures chosen for the spades are linked to digging and work.

Here's a reminder:

- Treat the ace as one: Its image will be connected with pens, paintbrushes, drawing, and painting.
- Two is linked with flying.
- Three is linked with the police.
- Four is linked to sailing.
- Five is linked to hooks and lifting.
- Six is linked to weaponry.
- Seven is linked to light.
- Eight is linked to snow and ice.
- Nine is linked to candy and food.
- Ten is linked to doors and buildings.
- The Jack is eleven, so its related images are connected with trains.
- The Queen is twelve, linked with clocks and time.
- Finally, the King is represented by the image of the suit itself: a heart, a diamond, a club, or a spade.

Read the image description of each playing card (overleaf) and bring each one to life in as much detail as possible. When you understand how each image links to the card, try recalling them all in order. After that, deal a real deck of cards and practice saying the associated images out loud.

WHAT'S OUR NUMBER?
Left and Below: Airplanes and clocks are vivid images used to remember playing card numbers. With this system, you can remember all 52 cards, boosting your playing confidence tremendously, as well as your observation skills and concentration span.

THE PLAYING CARD SYSTEM

Ace of hearts:
A poet
(heart suggests romance and one suggests writing).

Two of hearts:
An air stewardess
(heart suggests care, and two suggests flight).

Three of hearts:
Paramedic
(three could be extended from the police to other emergency services).

Four of hearts:
Romantic cruise ship.

Five of hearts:
Bride
(five can be a hook, suggesting getting hitched).

Six of hearts:
Cupid
(six is connected with weapons—here, Cupid's bow).

Seven of hearts:
Candle
(romantic lighting).

Eight of hearts:
Donor heart, packed in ice.

Nine of hearts:
Romantic meal.

Ten of hearts:
Church
(heart suggests marriage, and ten can be a building).

Jack of hearts:
Train fanatic.

Queen of hearts:
Heart pacemaker
(ticking like a clock, for twelve).

King of hearts:
A simple paper love heart.

Ace of spades:
Painter and decorator.

Two of spades:
Airline pilot.

Three of spades:
Police officer.

Four of spades:
Deckhand.

Five of spades:
Garbage collector.

Six of spades:
Soldier
(works with weapons).

Seven of spades:
Lighting technician.

Eight of spades:
Snow shovel.

Nine of spades:
Spoon
(think of it as a mini shovel for food).

Ten of spades:
Workmen's hut.

Jack of spades:
Coal shovel
(used on steam trains).

Queen of spades:
Workers' time clock.

King of spades:
Large garden spade.

Ace of clubs:
Crime novelist.

Two of clubs:
Majorette's baton, flying high in the air.

Three of clubs:
Police baton.

Four of clubs:
Pirate.

Five of clubs:
Pickpocket.

Six of clubs:
Armed robber.

Seven of clubs:
Searchlight, searching for escaped criminals.

Eight of clubs:
Snowball fight.

Nine of clubs:
Tray of prison food.

Ten of clubs:
Jailhouse.

Jack of clubs:
Train robber.

Queen of clubs:
Alarm clock
(picture the striking hammer).

King of clubs:
Caveman's large club.

Once you're familiar with the 52 images, you can put the system into action and try remembering some cards. Simply connect the appropriate images into a memorable storyline.

Ace of diamonds:
Diamond engraver.

Two of diamonds:
Diamond-encrusted jet.

Three of diamonds:
Diamond-covered bracelets.

Four of diamonds:
Luxury yacht.

Five of diamonds:
Miner, using a pick to search for diamonds.

Six of diamonds:
Jewel-encrusted handgun.

Seven of diamonds:
Jeweler's lamp.

Eight of diamonds:
A bucket of ice, sparkling like diamonds.

Nine of diamonds:
Caviar, one of the most expensive foods.

Ten of diamonds:
Palace covered with diamonds.

Jack of diamonds:
The Orient Express *(luxury train)*.

Queen of diamonds:
Jeweled wristwatch.

King of diamonds:
Huge diamond.

For example, to learn this sequence of cards (left), you might picture a soldier (card 1), wearing a jewel-encrusted wristwatch (card 2), tipping a bucket of ice (card 3) onto a pirate's (card 4) plate of caviar (card 5).

Use your imagination to extend the image possibilities for each card. The nine of diamonds, for example, could be any type of luxury food.

To remember this next series (below), you might imagine an air stewardess (card 1) changing a lightbulb (card 2) and replacing it with a paper love heart (card 3). Somehow, the light is now as bright as a searchlight (card 4), and it swings around to illuminate a luxury yacht (card 5).

Practice with small groups of cards until you're confident with the system, then try memorizing an entire pack. Divide the cards into nine groups of five, then turn each group into a memorable story or scene that can be fixed into a memory framework. In the tenth location, create a longer story to remember the final seven cards.

IMAGINATIVE THINKING

WHEN YOU OPEN YOUR MIND TO THE IMAGES, STORIES, AND PATTERNS INVOLVED IN MEMORY TECHNIQUES, YOUR THINKING TAKES ON NEW POWER. WHATEVER THE CHALLENGES FACED, YOU CAN EXPLORE THEM IN YOUR CREATIVE IMAGINATION, VIEW THEM FROM DIFFERENT ANGLES, AND IMAGINE SOLUTIONS WITH NEW-FOUND CONFIDENCE.

"RED HERRINGS" AND ASSUMPTIONS

Below: Always question "red herrings" and consensus opinions, as these can divert your logical train of thought and prevent solving problems. Assumptions are habitual pictures that appear in your mind and help form your ideas. Use your imagination to discard assumptions and consider everything afresh.

TRY THIS FOR STARTERS

Here is a famous lateral thinking question:

A man works on the top floor of a 20-story office block. In the evenings he takes the elevator to the ground floor, then goes home. In the mornings he returns to the building, enters the elevator, but usually gets out on the nineteenth floor and walks up the final flight of stairs to his apartment. Some days he manages to get all the way to the twentieth floor, but most of the time he takes this final walk. Why?

To help you solve the problem, bring your imagination into play. The trick is to avoid making assumptions. Mental pictures are an excellent resource, because you can begin by visualizing only the details you know are true, ensuring that you don't jump to the wrong conclusions. Add other details gradually, trying out possible scenarios, until you arrive at the best solution.

START AT THE BEGINNING

To tackle the elevator conundrum, begin by visualizing the details you know. Picture the high office block, and see the man taking the elevator

NEW PERSPECTIVES

Far Right: Visualizing the office block and elevator used in the lateral thinking story helps you explore queries in fresh ways, either for fun or in real-life situations.

down in the evening, then returning in the morning. You don't know what happens inside the elevator yet, so your "mental movie" must cut from him walking into the elevator to the moment when the doors open on the nineteenth or twentieth floor.

In fact, this is a vital discovery. Visualizing his day in this way highlights the gaps that you need to fill in—and the areas where the solution may lie.

What is different about the man's two journeys? Sometimes there might be other people in the elevator, so that could be a factor. Picture him pressing the button for the floor he wants. Imagine this in detail, and you'll see that the button for the ground floor is likely to be at the bottom of the panel, and the one for the twentieth floor at the very top. What might make him choose the nineteenth button instead on his way home?

Picture him reaching to the panel . . . what if he couldn't reach the twentieth button? Does that solution fit in with the rest of the puzzle? Play out this scenario—the man is just too short to reach the top button. Apart from the times when there's another passenger there to do it for him, he can only go as far as the nineteenth floor. That provides a solution to the puzzle.

CREATIVE THINKING

THE ABILITY TO DISCOVER, INVENT, AND EXPLAIN IS INTIMATELY
CONNECTED WITH THE ABILITY TO IMAGINE, WHICH IS AT THE
HEART OF ALL THE MEMORY STRATEGIES EXPLAINED IN THIS
BOOK. MANY OF HISTORY'S GREAT THINKERS RELIED ON
IMAGINATION TO MEET THE MENTAL CHALLENGES THEY FACED.

GENIUS THINKING
*Above: Although he was known
for furthering the cause of
science, Einstein said that
imagination was more important
than knowledge.*

$E=MC^2$

Albert Einstein once wrote: "My particular ability does not lie in mathematical calculation, but rather in visualizing effects, possibilities and consequences." It is known that he used his imagination to explore puzzling questions. He pictured himself riding on a beam of light and holding a clock when reasoning out the theory of relativity. The image of an elevator plummeting to the ground also helped him work out the full implications of his thoughts. He once went as far as to say that imagination was more important in his work than knowledge.

INSPIRATION IN THE FLAMES

The German chemist Kekulé was intent on discovering the molecular structure of benzene. Every night he sat in front of the fire, relaxing his mind as the patterns of the flames inspired him. He was in a dreamlike state of imaginary exploration when his key discovery was made:

"I turned my chair to the fire and dozed. Again the atoms were gamboling before my eyes. This time the smaller groups kept modestly in the background. My mental eye, rendered more acute by repeated visions of this kind, could now distinguish larger structures, in manifold conformation; long rows sometimes more closely fitted together, all turning and twisting in snakelike motion. But look! What was that? One of the snakes had seized hold of its own tail and the form whirled mockingly before my eyes. As if by a flash of lightning I awoke . . ."

The more you practice making mental images and manipulating

them in your mind, the easier it becomes to slip into this creative state. Since the information you're dealing with is also visual—again, the most memorable form—you won't forget your innovations and discoveries. Get used to turning everything into pictures; explore these pictures through the senses; experiment with fresh patterns; and be aware of the new possibilities your brain creates.

External Thinking Zones

It can also be effective to experiment with different external thinking zones, which will create different internal moods and patterns of thought. Just as Kekulé had his moment of inspiration in front of the fire, you need to find work spaces that allow your creative imagination to come to life.

Japan's Yoshiro NakaMats, one of history's most prolific inventors, carries out different stages of his creative process in well-defined settings. In a perfectly white room, his mind wanders and he explores new ideas. In what he calls a "creative swimming room," he engages in deep, focused interpretation of images and concepts. His inventions include the CD, floppy disks, and digital watches—and his 2,300-plus patents have made him a billionaire.

Do you Hear Music?
Above: Find your memory zone—the place where your brain works best. Experiment to find out if it's inside or out, a place with silence or with music, or a place where you're alone or with others.

Visualization to a T— Tesla's Imagination

The inventor Nikola Tesla honed his visualization skills so well that he could mentally construct any mechanism in intricate detail. Then, like a mental version of computer-aided design, he could view it from any angle and imagine exactly how it would perform when completed. His machinists reported that every measurement he produced came straight from his imagination—and that they were always accurate to within tiny fractions of an inch. Among Tesla's discoveries was the alternating current system of power generation, without which the age of electricity could not have come to pass.

That's Illogical

Max Planck, the father of quantum theory, wrote that any successful thinker must have "a vivid imagination for new ideas not generated by deduction but by artistically creative imagination." Seemingly logical problems can be solved within the playful, colorful, limitless, illogical imagination.

IMAGINATION AT WORK

YOUR TRAINED IMAGINATION CAN BE USED TO IMPROVE YOUR PERFORMANCE AT WORK.

Picture yourself at work, carrying out a key task. What do you see? It's likely that you see the exact same picture every time you think about your job. This is the framework you impose on work—and you can use it to improve your performance. You can take control of your mental pictures, altering the details to boost positive feelings.

STRESSED OUT?

If you're feeling stressed at work, make your visualization as relaxed as possible. In your mind, paint the walls in soothing colors, change the sounds and smells in the room, and spend time before and after work reinforcing this soothing perception. Rather than automatically picturing yourself in a difficult, stressful situation, you can change your habit to make the thought of work more appealing. You can also use controlled imagination to rehearse specific tasks—and to make useful additions to your strategies.

SCREEN SKILLS

If you work on a computer, visualize using it to enter, edit, retrieve, or process information. Picture the screen layouts and become familiar with this mental version of the real thing. In this way, you will speed up your computer skills through mental rehearsal and by feeling more confident about the software. In addition, you will find that you can perform many computer functions without having the terminal in front of you. For example, if you regularly check details of a client's account and happen to

need them when you're away from your computer, close your eyes and imagine what you would do to retrieve the details. You may well jog your memory to recall the information.

You might also try to process information, rather than just retrieve it. You may not be as accurate as a computer, but an imagined program can help you follow the right basic steps. If you are challenged to solve a problem, you can return to the computer in your mind to run the software.

The abacus—the ancient calculator made from beads and rods—is still used in some cultures. In contests, abacus experts perform amazing feats of calculation by simply visualizing an abacus to calculate answers.

PROGRESS TEST SIX

THESE TESTS DEVELOP THE SKILLS EXPLAINED IN THIS CHAPTER. CHOOSE YOUR FAVORITE FRAMEWORK AND USE IT TO SLOT IN THE INFORMATION AND CREATE MENTAL CLUES. PRACTICE RUNNING THROUGH THE FRAMEWORK BEFORE ATTEMPTING TO RETRIEVE THE VARIOUS PIECES OF INFORMATION.

CAMPING VACATION

HERE ARE SOME THINGS YOU MIGHT NEED TO REMEMBER WHEN PLANNING A CAMPING VACATION. FIX THE DETAILS IN YOUR MIND, THEN ANSWER THE QUESTIONS ON PAGE 140.

HOLIDAY DATES:
June 26th–July 5th.

Meet Alex at his house at 10 a.m.

THINGS TO BUY:
gas cylinders, matches, compass, flashlight, hiking boots.

IMPORTANT EXTRA THINGS TO PACK:
cutlery, water bottles, maps, insect repellent.

TELEPHONE NUMBER OF CAMPSITE:
3389021.

JEWELRY TALK

YOU ARE GIVING A TALK ON JEWELRY MAKING AND HAVE TO COVER TEN KEY POINTS (BELOW). FIX THE POINTS ONTO A MEMORY FRAMEWORK TO RECALL THEM LATER.

1 Tools   2 Materials   3 Ready-made extras   4 Band rings   5 Ornate rings

6 Using beads   7 Pendants   8 Stone setting   9 Bangles   10 Twisted wire

JOB SATISFACTION

THINK OF A REGULAR WORK TASK FOR TWO MINUTES, THEN ALTER TEN THINGS ABOUT IT TO MAKE IT MORE ATTRACTIVE. REHEARSE THE TASK AGAIN FOR A MINUTE, THINKING OF THE MOTIVATION BEHIND YOUR CHANGES. FINISH BY ADDING THREE EXTRA-FAMILIAR DETAILS TO MAKE THE IMAGE MORE MEMORABLE.

PLAYING CARDS

TAKE FIVE MINUTES TO LEARN THIS SEQUENCE OF PLAYING CARDS: TURN EACH CARD INTO ITS ASSIGNED IMAGE, THEN CREATE A STRONG STORYLINE WHICH CONNECTS THE RELEVANT IMAGES.

HOW WELL DID YOU DO?

CAN YOU ANSWER THE FOLLOWING QUESTIONS FROM MEMORY? JOT DOWN YOUR ANSWERS, AND CHECK YOUR SUCCESS BY REFERRING TO THE PREVIOUS PAGE.

CAMPING VACATION

TRY ANSWERING THESE QUESTIONS.

1 **What five things do you need to buy for this trip?**

_____

_____

_____

_____

_____

2 **On what day will you be coming home?**

_____

3 **What time are you meeting Alex on June 26th?**

_____

4 **What is the telephone number of the campsite?**

_____

5 **What would be missing if you packed the following items?**

Blankets, flashlight, maps, books, tent, insect repellent, cutlery, toiletries.

_____

_____

JEWELRY TALK

SEE HOW MANY OF THE POINTS YOU CAN WRITE DOWN FROM MEMORY.

PLAYING CARDS

CALL OUT, OR WRITE DOWN, THE SEQUENCE OF TEN PLAYING CARDS IN THEIR CORRECT ORDER. SLOWLY REPLAY THE STORYLINE IN YOUR MIND'S EYE IN ORDER TO RETRIEVE THE ASSIGNED IMAGES AND THEIR ASSOCIATED CARD SUITS AND NUMBERS.

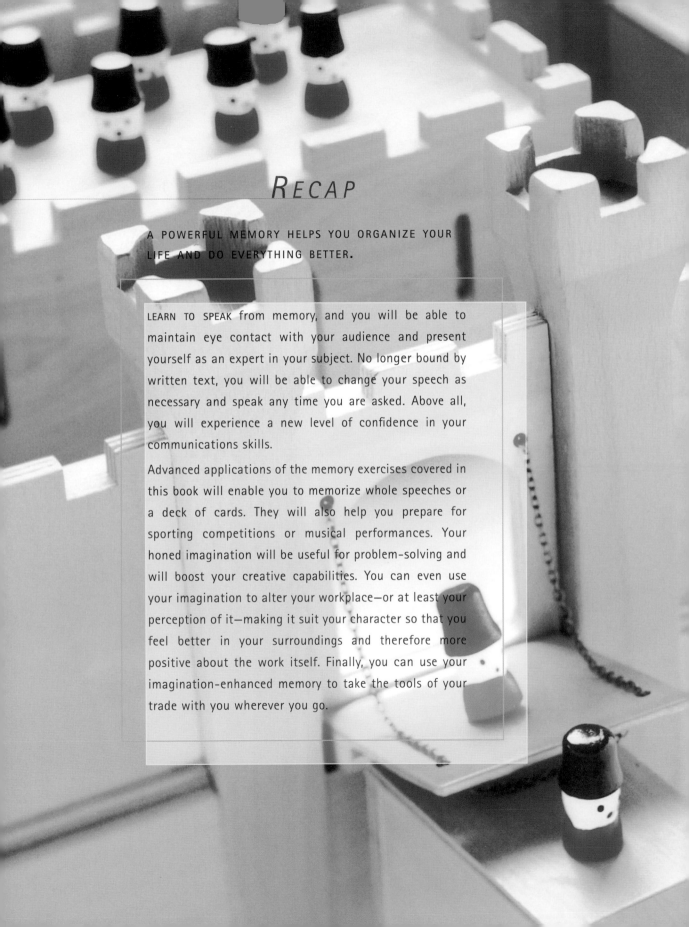

RECAP

A POWERFUL MEMORY HELPS YOU ORGANIZE YOUR LIFE AND DO EVERYTHING BETTER.

LEARN TO SPEAK from memory, and you will be able to maintain eye contact with your audience and present yourself as an expert in your subject. No longer bound by written text, you will be able to change your speech as necessary and speak any time you are asked. Above all, you will experience a new level of confidence in your communications skills.

Advanced applications of the memory exercises covered in this book will enable you to memorize whole speeches or a deck of cards. They will also help you prepare for sporting competitions or musical performances. Your honed imagination will be useful for problem-solving and will boost your creative capabilities. You can even use your imagination to alter your workplace—or at least your perception of it—making it suit your character so that you feel better in your surroundings and therefore more positive about the work itself. Finally, you can use your imagination-enhanced memory to take the tools of your trade with you wherever you go.

MEMORY EXERCISES FOR DAILY LIFE

AN EXERCISED MIND CAN STAY FIT AND ACTIVE ALL YOUR LIFE. THE EXPERIENCE OF REMEMBERING CHANGES WITH AGE, BUT YOU CAN LEARN TO ACCOMMODATE MEMORY CHANGES, WHATEVER YOUR LIFESTYLE. MOST IMPORTANTLY, YOU CAN ENJOY THE DELIGHTS OF MEMORY: THE PAST CAN INFORM YOU, KEEP YOU COMPANY, AND ENRICH THE PRESENT.

MEMORY AND AGING

ONE OF THE MOST FASCINATING AREAS OF
MEMORY RESEARCH IS DEVOTED TO THE
CHANGING EXPERIENCE OF REMEMBERING.

It is clear that when an 89-year-old remembers what it
was like to be 88, he or she has a very different
experience from that of a nine-year-old thinking back
one year. Likewise, a 70-year-old's ability to learn new
information differs greatly from that of a teenager. Still,
the general belief that memory simply deteriorates with
age is wrong. Memory changes, but the outlook is far
more hopeful than most people would believe.

As children, we have little responsibility, and we're
seldom expected to remember much. We can recall the
past, but our ability to distinguish between important
and trivial events is limited. What we do
learn, we learn quickly, but we also tend
to forget quickly. Prospective memory—
especially about events we're excitedly
looking forward to—is likely to be strong.

As adults, we're required to acquire
and retain much more information. We
also have to live with the consequences
of forgetting. The older we get, the
longer it takes to learn, but we're also
less likely to forget the things we *have*
learned. We can distinguish between
important and trivial memories, although
prospective memory seems to get
significantly worse with age.

MEMORY BAG
*Below: You may sometimes feel as
if your memories are so unreliable
that they resemble loose items
tossed randomly into a grocery
bag. This negative perception can
be reversed as soon as you start to
employ memory systems in
everyday life.*

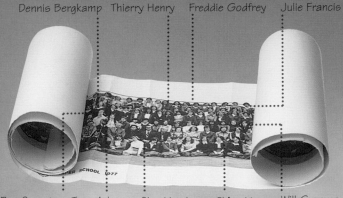

Dennis Bergkamp Thierry Henry Freddie Godfrey Julie Francis

Ray Coventry Tony Adams Oleg Lhuzhny Ch'en Ling Will Greaves

CHILDREN'S MEMORIES
Above: Children find it hard to prioritize their memory. For example, they may recall what games the other children in their class like to play—but may completely forget their names.

CHANGES IN MEMORY

Over the course of a lifetime, a number of physical factors influence our memories. For women, changes in hormone levels can have dramatic effects on information recall. The areas of the brain involved in

YOUR MEMORY LIFE CYCLE
Main Picture: Different stages in physical development correspond with different memory experiences. Think of your memory as "changing" rather than failing. Remember that many prescription drugs and medical procedures can cause short-lived memory problems, so it's always worthwhile asking your doctor whether there are alternatives you could try.

memory require a constant supply of the female hormone estrogen, and many women report memory problems just before the menstrual phase of the reproductive cycle, when estrogen levels are lowest, as well as following menopause. Although age-related conditions such as Alzheimer's disease have fundamental effects on memory, a decline in mental function and recall ability is not a normal part of age. During their fifties and sixties, most people notice a marked change in certain areas of memory—particularly the abilities to learn new information and keep upcoming events in mind—while memories of the distant past remain strong. By keeping their brains active, using the strategies explained in this book to learn new information, and applying wisdom and experience to fill in any gaps in recall, older people can maintain total confidence in their powers of memory.

LIFELONG LEARNING

"USE IT OR LOSE IT." IT SOUNDS LIKE A CLICHÉ, BUT IT'S TRUE: THE MORE YOU CHALLENGE YOUR MIND, THE FITTER IT STAYS. RESEARCH HAS SHOWN THAT EVEN PATIENTS WITH ALZHEIMER'S DISEASE CAN REMEMBER CHANGES IN ROUTINE, DAYS OUT, AND SPECIAL OCCASIONS. MEMORY NEEDS TO BE STIMULATED TO KEEP WORKING.

PAY ATTENTION

As eighteenth-century English author and scholar Samuel Johnson wrote, "The true art of memory is the art of attention." You can't learn or remember if you haven't focused on the material that you need to retain. Make sure you have no vision or hearing problems that could interfere with your attentiveness. Many people wrongly believe their memories are failing when in fact their senses simply aren't picking up all the messages they need to recall.

RADIO WAVES

Above: A good old-fashioned radio station is still one of the best memory aids you can get, telling you the time and giving up-to-date news throughout the day.

USE MEMORY AIDS

Diaries, calendars, organizers, and other people can help you keep hold of information. A couple of words in a diary entry can kindle a faint recollection into a glowing blaze of memory. Memory aids are status symbols of a sort for busy young people, so there is no reason to assume that they're props for an aging mind. Use them consistently, keep them in the same place and refer to them regularly—this way they will provide a powerful foundation for organizing your memories.

TODAY'S TECHNOLOGY

Right: Lap-top and palm-top computers are the memory aids of today, and can hold immense quantities of information. If you need to empty your own mind of excess data, just download onto your preferred piece of technology to make room for new entries.

STRETCH YOUR BRAIN

If a particular memory won't come back, pursue it until it does. Get into the habit of expecting success from your memory, and challenge yourself to recapture faded information. For instance, return to the place you were standing or to the task you were doing when

you last thought of something, or follow a pattern of associations in your mind until you arrive at the information you need. Stay in touch with what it feels like to remember, and keep your memory working.

KEEP YOUR IMAGINATION ALIVE

Reading novels, listening to the radio, writing poetry, and painting are all excellent ways of looking after the imagination. Aristotle believed it was impossible to think without evoking a mental picture. Whatever your age, make use of your experiences and travels to flesh out imagery for the memory strategies explained in this book. Memory works best if you use it in the most natural way. Seek out new things to learn, but keep up all the good mental habits.

REMEMBER YOUR DREAMS

The students in a class were challenged to talk about their dreams every week. They each had to discuss their dreams and possible meanings with the rest of the class. To begin with, many of the students said they remembered few, if any, of their dreams. After a few weeks of the term, however, they were all consistently coming up with detailed dreams. Interestingly, they were also doing considerably better in their other classes, taking up more

hobbies, and reporting positive changes in their social lives—as well as in their mood and outlook on life.

We all dream every night we fall asleep. If you designate one of your memory frameworks as a "dream store," you may be able to remember more of your dreams. As soon as you wake up, pick a few key images from your dream and fix them into the framework. Get into the habit of doing this, and review your storehouse regularly.

DREAM STATES

Above: " 'Oh, I've had such a curious dream!' said Alice." Lewis Carroll's classic story Alice's Adventures in Wonderland *ends with Alice's realization that her experiences were part of a dream. Take stock of the images in your dreams, as they will help you retain your imaginative qualities and keep your mind active.*

SLEEP, DIET, EXERCISE

REST AND SLEEP

It's easy to assume that the most important mental activity takes place during periods of intense study—but consider how many of your best ideas and most powerful recollections have occurred to you during moments of repose. The Greek philosopher Archimedes shouted "Eureka!" while sitting in his bath, and British physicist Isaac Newton was reputedly resting in his garden when he formulated his theory of gravitation. Both of these men were inspired by the things around them—Archimedes by the water and Newton by a falling apple—and it's likely that a state of relaxation made them particularly receptive. In the same way, you'll find that "lost" memories often return to you when your mind is calm and unconcerned with that particular question. Your brain requires regular rest to be at its best; therefore, you should never think of rest as time wasted. Make the most of the times when your mind wanders into daydreams.

Regular sleep patterns are also important to good memory function. Different people need different amounts of sleep, but we all know when we haven't slept enough. Sleep may serve as a time for solving problems, gaining perspective, resting and rejuvenating the mind, so its importance should never be underestimated. If you have difficulty sleeping, take all possible steps to remedy the situation. Your memory simply won't work without enough regular sleep.

EXERCISE

Aerobic exercise has been shown to improve the quality of sleep. Lack of exercise can lead to erratic sleeping patterns and actually increase your sleep requirements. Stay physically active, and your sleep is likely to be restorative and enjoyable. Why? Partly because a fit person can process up to twice as much oxygen as someone who is out of shape.

TAKE IT EASY
Main Picture: Sir Isaac Newton conceived the idea of universal gravitation after seeing an apple fall from a tree in his garden in 1665. The very fact that he was enjoying a relaxing experience when the idea struck highlights the importance of relaxation as a means to improve the mind and memory. You could designate a mental framework to hold the ideas you have during restful periods for retrieval later.

KEEP ACTIVE
Right: A healthy body is essential for a healthy mind.

Therefore, the more active you are, the better your brain's supply of oxygen will be. Your brain accounts for only about three percent of your overall body weight, but it can use as much as half of the oxygen you take in.

DIET

A balanced diet is essential to good memory, to provide the brain with all the nutrients it needs. Some key substances are especially important for mental function:

LECITHIN, found in fish, egg yolks, wheat and soybeans, seems to be the key to keeping a memory working well. Lecithin breaks down into choline, and experiments have shown that it can boost memory power significantly.

GLUTAMIC ACID, found in dairy products, whole wheat, and soybeans, is a powerful brain fuel.

PHENYLALANINE, another amino acid found in meats, milk, cheese, and eggs, is one of the materials the brain uses to make norepinephrine, a substance vital to the memory process.

RIBONUCLEIC ACID (RNA) is thought to extend the life of brain cells. It is found in seafood, which also contains dimethyl-amino-ethanol, a substance used in the manufacture of the chemicals that transmit electrical messages throughout the brain. It is more than an old wives' tale that fish is brain food.

Some medications affect memory, so it's worth checking with your doctor if you notice changes in your powers of recall while taking certain drugs. Nutritional supplements that claim to boost memory are also on the market now. Among these are derivatives of the ginkgo tree, a 200-million-year-old species used in China for around three thousand years. Other herbs believed to boost memory are sage, rosemary, and lemon balm.

Recent research shows that maintaining normal blood-sugar levels is important for thinking your best. Eating plenty of small meals during the day may be more beneficial to memory than sitting down to two or three large ones.

CONSULT YOUR DOCTOR
Below: Your doctor may be able to suggest alternative drugs if you experience changes in your memory capabilities.

EAT WELL
Left: Keep up your vitamin and mineral levels with at least five portions of fresh fruit and vegetables per day. Minimize your intake of fat, salt, and sugars, which can be very high in convenience food.

REMEMBERING THE PAST

The older we get, the more our memories focus on the distant past. Although short-term recall may feel weak, our ability to remember moments from childhood seems stronger than ever. One reason we have such vivid powers of recall for past events is that we have rehearsed these memories again and again. This continual review, however, also means that their accuracy may be doubtful. Exploring the long-term memory can be therapeutic and comforting, but it can also give rise to more than a few surprises.

Pick an early memory that you have thought about and perhaps described to others. Close your eyes, and let this distant moment fill your mind, including as many details as possible. Now, no matter how real this memory seems, ask yourself how much of it really happened.

RETELLING THE PAST

Many people find that their early memories are a mixture of various elements: actual events, photographs, family stories, and idealized versions. The "Chinese whispers" effect, by which information is changed slightly with each retelling, plays an important role here. It has been said that a memory isn't as much a recollection of an actual event as a recollection of the last time you remembered it. You might alter a memory slightly, then

MAKING THE MOST OF TIME
Main Picture: Spend a few minutes every day reflecting on distant memories, and you'll keep your memory sharp while making the past part of your positive approach to the present and the future.

confidently recall the altered version at a later date. Further alterations may follow. You may feel sure that a particular memory is accurate, but investigation can uncover any number of inaccuracies and impossibilities. Ask other people who were involved in the event, and consult diary entries and old photographs for verification. You might see that your memories of the past are not as fixed and permanent as perhaps you thought.

Three days after the explosion of the Challenger space shuttle, which occurred on January 28, 1986, memory researchers asked a number of volunteers to recall where they were when they learned about the tragedy. Nine months later, the volunteers were asked to recount their memories again.

The result: There were some major discrepancies between the two retellings. In the intervening months, many of the memories had changed dramatically. Some of the volunteers placed themselves with different people in the two versions; sometimes they recalled being in completely different places.

TIME TRAVEL

Of course, many of your distant memories will be highly accurate, and you can use your trained mind to "time travel." Start by relaxing

fully and awakening your imagination (see the exercise on page 43). Next, pick a single detail of a memory from long ago, and see what else it sparks in your mind. Let associations flow freely among remembered images and sensations.

If learning from experience is important, then this type of time travel is the perfect way to remember past successes and failures, and to make the most of the knowledge they have given you. The unfixed nature of these memories means that you can also manipulate them inside your imagination, emphasizing the specific things you want to remember and minimizing things you would rather forget.

SHARING THE PAST
Below: Anecdotal evidence suggests that regularly sharing your memories and recalling events from the past helps to maintain your memory power.

TACTICS FOR RECOVERING MEMORIES

Witness testimony can be crucial to legal proceedings, so it's not surprising that research has been done to find the best ways to trigger a witness's memory. In one interesting study, carried out by Fisher and Geiselman in 1988, four key strategies were highlighted. Whenever a particular event or piece of information proves elusive, try the following tactics to recapture it.

STEP ONE: GO BACK TO THE EVENT

Use your imagination to take you back to the event you're trying to remember.

Witnesses are encouraged to recreate as many of the original "conditions" as possible. What was the weather like? What were you wearing? How did you feel?

Whenever your memory seems sluggish, try to refocus your mind on the moment when you learned a particular piece of information. Sometimes, just remembering where you were is enough to jog your memory. Memory is often dependent on context—for example, it is common to meet someone you know in an unusual setting and have trouble figuring out who they are—so try to recreate as much of the event's context as possible, including psychological conditions such as your mood and level of alertness or fatigue. People under the influence of alcohol often have difficulty remembering what they did when they were drunk—until the next time they drink, when the original context is restored. Your trained imagination lets you return to the moment when information was first taken in.

CONDITIONS TO REMEMBER:	
Weather?	Raining
Clothing?	Suit and shirt
Mood?	OK, Bar in sight
Company?	Linda, Sue
Discussed?	New secretary
Food?	Burger
Odd events?	Hare Krishna
Traffic?	Cycle couriers

STEP TWO: CONCENTRATE ON DETAILS

Try to focus on all the details, even those that seem irrelevant. Witnesses often find that their memories improve when they highlight a detail of the events, then follow a chain of associations. If only part of a memory comes back to you, let even the seemingly unimportant details provide you with a starting point, then see where the associations take you.

VITAL CLUES
The keys, cars, and dog are clues in this chain.

STEP THREE: THE MENTAL PICTURES IN A DIFFERENT SEQUENCE

For an eyewitness to a robbery, this might mean starting with the moment the robbers ran out of sight and reviewing the elements of the crime backwards. After a traffic accident, witnesses might be asked to describe the two cars hitting each other, and then explain what happened before and after. If you find that some images have disappeared from your memory, work through the clues in reverse.

ACCIDENT SCENE
Where injury or crime is involved, the memory may shut down more than usual due to shock.

STEP FOUR: CHANGE THE PERSPECTIVE

Describe an incident from several different viewpoints. What would the robbery have looked like through the robber's eyes, or from the point of view of someone walking on the other side of the street? How might the crash have appeared from inside one of the cars, or from a helicopter hovering above?

Within mental frameworks, your mind's eye can change position and view items from different angles. In real life, too, your imagination can give you a new perspective. If you lost something at work, for example, you could visualize your movements through someone else's eyes, and recall the one place you hadn't checked.

EVERY ANGLE
Look at a situation from all angles for extra insight.

GLOBAL THINKING

THE ULTIMATE AIM OF ALL THE STRATEGIES IN THIS BOOK IS TO ENCOURAGE GLOBAL THINKING, THE MOST EFFECTIVE, EFFICIENT, AND ENJOYABLE LEVEL OF MENTAL FUNCTION. WHEN YOU THINK GLOBALLY, YOUR WHOLE MIND WORKS TO ONE END.

YOUR TWO BRAINS
Below: The most effective memory techniques use both the right and left sides of the brain.

The character of memory changes with age throughout life, but the natural strategies of global thinking can be combined in one powerful, unchanging approach. Use your memory the same way some of history's greatest thinkers used theirs, and you can maintain an astounding level of brain power.

In the 1960s, California professor Roger Sperry identified a crucial aspect of mental function that forms a basis for the concept of global thinking. He demonstrated that the human brain is actually *two* brains since there are vital differences between the right and left sides.

The right brain is dominant in imaginative thinking. It loves pictures, colors and shapes, and produces ideas and dreams. The left brain is dominant in matters of logic. It processes words, numbers, and lists; it analyzes and checks; it makes rational decisions.

Since that time, research into the two sides of the brain has revealed that the most successful thinkers combine the logical and intuitive regions, using the whole brain to achieve *global* thinking. By using the skills explained in this book, you too have been bringing both sides into play at once.

In the best memory strategies, imaginative, colorful, fun pictures (right side) are fitted into ordered patterns and frameworks (left side). Exploring the images through instinctive patterns of association (right side) allows you to draw rational conclusions and make planned, logical decisions (left side).

You might also say that global

thinking combines childlike and adult patterns of thought in a single approach to learning. Children learn naturally by being inquisitive and imaginative. Their books and lessons encourage them to think in pictures and stories, and their right brain dominates.

With age, the left brain takes over. Learning materials become logical, so that as adults we tend to approach new information in highly unimaginative ways. Some of us have a natural bias to right or left depending on our interests and character, but in general terms, an "adult" approach is left-brained, missing out on many of the benefits of right-brain activity. Separately, the two sides are incomplete. Children may learn quickly, but their thinking tends to be disorganized. They have difficulty structuring and prioritizing information. Adults think in a more orderly way, but they can find it difficult to make judgments, use their senses, and learn and explore new material imaginatively.

These contrasting approaches to learning are incredibly powerful. Many of the greatest and most famous thinkers in history illustrate global thinking in action.

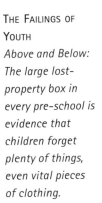

THE FAILINGS OF YOUTH
Above and Below: The large lost-property box in every pre-school is evidence that children forget plenty of things, even vital pieces of clothing.

WOLFGANG AMADEUS MOZART

In the book *Extraordinary Minds*, Howard Gardner points out that Mozart was enthusiastic about mathematics and languages as well as music. His character seems to have been an exciting mix of the right- and left-brain principles.

"Mozart represented an extreme in the amalgam of the young and foolish on the one hand, and the mature and wise on the other. All Masters (indeed, all creators) combine the childlike and adultlike—indeed many feel that this fusion constitutes an indispensable aspect of their genius," Gardner writes.

Mozart was, by instinct, a global thinker, and we know that his memory was amazing. On one occasion, while still a boy, he listened to Gregorio Allegri's *Miserere*, a complex sacred piece that could not, by church dictates, be removed from the chapel where it was stored. He transcribed it entirely from memory. A scholar later checked Mozart's accuracy, and found just one, tiny mistake.

GIFTED FROM CHILDHOOD
Mozart could listen to a piece of music once, then reconstruct it from memory, note for note.

ALBERT EINSTEIN

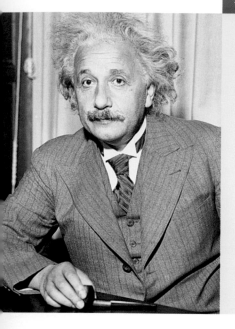

Einstein was expelled from school for disruption. Despite his apparent absent-mindedness, he had an incredibly inquisitive mind. Through his life, he was fascinated by many topics and pursuits—in later life he played the violin and sailed.

Einstein combined imaginative thinking with rational analysis to make his great discoveries. He drew conclusions about the universe that provided him with the foundations for many groundbreaking theories. Picturing himself riding on a beam of light at the speed of light helped him towards his most famous equation of all: $E = MC^2$, the theory of relativity.

DAYDREAM BELIEVER
Einstein described a daydream in which he was riding a sunbeam to the end of the universe—and found that, at "the end," he was back where he started.

LEWIS CARROLL

A mathematics professor at Christ Church, Oxford, Lewis Carroll—real name Charles Dodgson—wrote books and papers on logic. He also wrote the ultimate fantasy novel, a masterpiece of bizarre images and illogical happenings: *Alice's Adventures in Wonderland*.

Alice is a mixture of right- and left-brain thinking. The title character's strange journey follows a clear pattern, but it is a pattern that often makes no sense. Full of freakish, colorful characters, humor, violence, senses, and strong emotions, it is a great example of childlike thinking and highlights the importance of logic. Carroll was fascinated by memory. He wrote several papers on it, and the *Alice* books easily lodge themselves in readers' memories.

MAGICAL IMAGES
The White Rabbit is an enduring vision of childhood imagination, as characterized in Carroll's classic fantasy stories.

LEONARDO DA VINCI

The man who painted the *Mona Lisa* also sketched flying machines and tanks, designs that survive in his notebooks, demonstrating his particular approach to global thinking.

Leonardo's artworks were created with great attention to technical detail. His notes, which indicate that he employed controlled light sources, show an understanding of physics. He also made detailed records of the exact colors required for different areas of each painting, taking a highly rational approach to the creative process.

His technical diagrams, on the other hand, are highly artistic and imaginative. The four key principles he identified sum up his genius:

1 Study the art of science

2 Study the science of art

3 Learn to see and to use all your senses

4 Study in the knowledge that everything connects

REACH NEW LEVELS OF THINKING
Let your brain's impulses toward order and randomness work together and overlap. This way you will access astonishing learning power.

REVOLUTIONIZE YOUR LIFE

NOW THAT YOU KNOW HOW MEMORY WORKS AND HOW TO TAKE ADVANTAGE OF ITS INCREDIBLE POWERS, IT'S TIME TO DO SOMETHING ABOUT IT. ADAPT YOUR NEW SKILLS TO SUIT YOUR NEEDS. SET PERSONAL GOALS FOR YOUR FUTURE DEVELOPMENT AND START INTRODUCING OTHER PEOPLE TO THE BENEFITS OF IMPROVED MEMORY. YOUR MEMORY CAN HELP YOU MAKE A REAL IMPACT ON THE WORLD, LETTING YOU STAND OUT AND BE NOTICED AS A TRUE INDIVIDUAL.

REMEMBERING TO REMEMBER

TO MANAGE TIME EFFECTIVELY, YOU NEED TO KEEP TRACK OF CHORES AND RESPONSIBILITIES. HERE YOU'LL FIND OUT HOW TO SORT JOBS INTO MEMORABLE LISTS AND REMEMBER THEM AT THE RIGHT TIME.

We've all had the experience of packing up to leave work, only to find one final job that has still to be done. Worse yet, if the job had been done at the right time, it would have taken maybe ten minutes; now, it's going to take an hour.

CHOOSE A SPECIAL PLACE

If you find yourself forgetting everyday jobs, try designing a specific store dedicated to memory. Choose a place you see every day— your neighbor's house, for example, or a supermarket or a church you can see from your

MEMORY REHEARSAL
Below: Think of the regular chores you forget to do most often then prioritize these in your "remembering to remember" system. For example, returning library books, feeding the cat, or picking up your dry-cleaning.

than dividing this place into ten areas, think of it as a single space into which to place images.

Every time you think of a task, design an image to represent it. Exaggerate your picture, then fix it into place in your mental store in the most memorable way possible.

You might picture yourself nailing a heavy bag of groceries to the ceiling as a reminder to do the shopping. To remember to deposit your pay-check, you could imagine papering an entire wall with checks.

Mentally return to your "things to do" memory store throughout the day, and check the picture clues you've left. Crucially, you should always think about your list every time you pass the *real* location. That way, you'll check your memory regularly; in time it will become a habit. As soon as you have completed a task, you can remove its image. Use visualization to imagine pulling out the nails holding the grocery bag, or scraping the checks off the wall. The picture clues need only stay there until they have served their purpose.

KEEP USING YOUR IMAGINATION

Your imagination can also prompt you to carry out tasks at particular times. Visualize where you'll be when the time to shop or make a phone call arrives, and focus on a particular detail of that location—something you're bound to notice. Next, create an image to remind you of the task you want to remember. Connect this image with your detail in an imaginative way.

Perhaps you think of a golf ball shooting out at you from a friend's grandfather clock, reminding you to ask him about your next game. If you imagine pieces of broken glass spilling out of a shopping cart, you will remember to buy lightbulbs the next time you go to the supermarket. Picture

To Do
Fax to Elizabeth ✔
Call Judith ✔
Courier to Julie ✔
Finish artwork ✔
Buy dog food ✔
Chase invoice ✔
Photocopy files ✔
Back-up disk ✔

yourself standing in the place in question and spotting the key detail, which will then surprise you by becoming the picture clue. Try to imagine the context: How will you be feeling when you're there, and what will the images remind you to do? Bring as much emotion as you can to your visualization, and rehearse the way this strategy will actually work.

When you find yourself in the real location, you'll have a sense that there is something you need to remember. You'll spot the key detail, and it will trigger your memory to release the image.

Say you are sitting in your friend's house and you spot his grandfather clock. If you've done your visualization you will remember the golf ball hitting you in the face, and you'll know what to discuss.

DESIGN A STOREHOUSE
Left: Create a special place in your mind to keep track of all the odd jobs you need to do in a single day. For example, you could visualize a memo board, a familiar building, or even a simple box.

MAKE YOURSELF MEMORABLE

IN MANY SITUATIONS, IT'S NOT ENOUGH TO HAVE A
GOOD MEMORY YOURSELF; IT'S ALSO VITAL THAT
OTHER PEOPLE REMEMBER YOU AS WELL.

Once you know how to develop a powerful memory, you
can use your skills to fix yourself in other people's
memories. The result: You'll make a lasting impression at
job interviews, form and maintain strong relationships,
lead effective meetings, and give presentations that stick
with your listeners. Just observe the following ten rules:

1 HELP PEOPLE REMEMBER YOUR NAME

Make sure that the people you meet
hear your name properly, a catchy
comment can help them remember
it. Perhaps you have the same name
as a mutual friend. You might have
a famous namesake. You could spell
your name, explain what it means,
or make a joke about it. Before
parting, repeat important points and
always give new work acquaintances
your business card as an extra
memory jogger.

WHAT'S IN A NAME
*Your name defines and identifies you—
always make sure people remember it.*

2 SPEAK IN PICTURES

Great orators have always used striking images, similes, and metaphors to make their words memorable. People tend to forget abstract explanations, so give key concepts images instead. Making a presentation, you might describe how something works, allowing your audience to picture the process. Alternatively, you can liken one object to another. Think of how children's pictures, parables, and fables present complex ideas in simple ways.

USE CREATIVE IMAGES
To explain a medical condition, a doctor might make an analogy between the progress of a disease and an advancing enemy army, held back by the soldier-like cells of the body.

3 GIVE YOUR WORDS STRUCTURE

Imagery and sensory information activate your audience's right brain, but an organized idea structure is necessary to engage the left brain as well. Always present ideas in a logical order. If the people listening to you lose the thread of what you're saying, they won't remember it.

PROVIDE MENTAL FILE CARDS
Guide your audience through the framework of your talk, rather than leaving them to unravel the information.

4 EXCITE YOUR AUDIENCE'S EMOTIONS

Memory is strongly connected to feelings, so it's important to excite as many emotions in your audience as possible. Include humor, surprise, and perhaps something inspirational. A relaxed but attentive mood is most conducive.

MAKE IT FUN
Do everything you can to engage your listeners in what they're hearing, employing original props if appropriate.

5 PRESENT INFORMATION IN A VARIETY OF WAYS

Some people learn best by seeing information; others learn by hearing. Give your audience several options for taking in what you have to say. If you use visual aids, make them simple, striking, and memorable. Consider using audio aids as well.

MIXED MEDIA
Present information in a variety of different ways.

6 PAY ATTENTION TO THE RHYTHMS OF MEMORY

Your audience will be most receptive at the start and end of a presentation. It's wise to make the most of these times to get your points across. Minds may start to wander halfway through your talk, so put extra effort into reinforcing what you say at this time.

DURING A
PRESENTATION
When your listeners' minds wander, double your efforts to activate their memories.

7 REHEARSE YOUR PERFORMANCE

People will remember you more readily if you impress them as being confident, knowledgeable, and fluent. Always try to deliver your information from memory, and practice important presentations in front of a mirror or camcorder.

THINK IT, DO IT
Rehearse in front of a camcorder or mirror to help you perfect your performance.

8 MAKE YOUR HANDOUTS MEMORABLE

Consider the documents that you give—handouts, minutes, or notes. If people are going to remember the content of your documents, memory principles should apply to these too. Make sure everything is clear, and the key points are highlighted with color and imagery.

MAKE IT READABLE
Make your handouts attractive and accessible.

9 MOTIVATE PEOPLE TO REMEMBER YOU

Give the listeners clear reasons for putting in the mental effort to remember what you have to say. Perhaps you can help them make money, stay safe, save time, or pass exams. Boost your audience's motivation before you start, to spark their interest, and reiterate the motivating principles again at the end.

EMPHASIZE THE BENEFITS
If there is a reward, such as money or a certificate, your words are sure to be remembered.

10 PROVIDE MEMORY CUES FOR FUTURE USE

If you help other people learn effectively, you should only have to give simple reminders later on for all the information to come rushing back. If people you've met previously don't remember you instantly, make it easy for them: Simply tell them your name again and remind them about your earlier meeting. Use the fact that *you* can remember to help them remember too.

GIVING THE CUE
Pick the most memorable factors to help trigger recall.

ADVERTISE YOURSELF

These ten rules help you advertise yourself. Advertisers know that the human memory can be easily activated and controlled. When you watch a TV commercial or read a big-budget magazine ad, you should be able to pick out many examples of memorable communications. All day, every day, we are bombarded with messages full of strong images, humor, surprise, and emotion. Advertisers tap into our memories without our realizing it—and you can use many of the same techniques to market yourself as you want to be remembered.

Decide how you want other people to think of you, then make sure that you present these sides of yourself in the most memorable way possible. At a job interview, for example, you could tell a vivid story about a particular achievement, creating images and evoking emotions and ensuring that you are remembered for your most notable past successes.

THE WAY AHEAD

ONCE YOU KNOW HOW TO REMEMBER,
YOU SIMPLY HAVE TO START DOING IT.

Thinking is habitual, and your old patterns may take a while to break.
Go slowly and implement new techniques gradually. Your new approach
may well feel unnatural for a while. With patience, though, the strategies
in this book will become instinctive and replace the bad habits of the past.

AT THE START OF EVERY DAY . . .

- Spend a few moments remembering your
  dreams (see page 147). Relax your mind, focus
  on the images and events that you can recall,
  and consider whether you can learn
  anything from them for the coming day.
  Fix any particularly meaningful or useful
  images into a familiar memory framework.

- Use your trained imagination to visualize the day ahead. Remind
  yourself of the key challenges you face, and picture yourself meeting
  them successfully. Highlight any fears or worries, and work on
  altering your mental pictures to boost positive emotions.

- Check your mental storehouse for
  important tasks (see pages 160–161).

- Create picture reminders for any tasks
  or facts you might easily forget
  (see page 161).

IN THE COURSE OF THE DAY . . .

- Regularly consult your mental storehouse to complete all the necessary tasks.

- Make the most of your powers of recall to remember the following:
  Names and faces (see page 87).
  PIN codes, telephone numbers and dates (see pages 74–77).
  New skills and procedures (see pages 78–79).
  Directions (see pages 98–101).

AT THE END OF THE DAY . . .

- Decide what new information you need to know for the future, particularly names and faces, and create extra memory triggers to keep the memories strong.

- Focus on tasks to complete the following day, and create new images to add to your mental storehouse.

- Spend a few moments preparing for coming challenges, mentally rehearsing your approach and establishing the best frame of mind.

- Use your controlled imagination to completely relax your mind, and prepare for creative, inspirational, memorable dreams.

FINAL PROGRESS TEST

THE AIM OF THIS SEVENTH, AND FINAL, TEST
IS TO GAUGE YOUR PROGRESS SINCE THE FIRST
ASSESSMENT ON PAGES 17–18.

In reading this book, you have experienced a range
of memory skills, all of which require you to use your
imagination. Now is your chance to find out whether
the key techniques are part of your everyday life.

Think about how far you have come since you
were first introduced to memory techniques: the fun
you have had using stories and images to store
information, the creation of personalized mental
frameworks based on real life or fantasy locations,
and applying visual references to every piece of data
you need to remember. Before you start the test,
revise the skills taught so far. Don't be panicked by
the finality of the test—this is just the beginning of
your new memory lifestyle: confident and great fun.

NAMES AND FACES

YOU HAVE TWO MINUTES TO STUDY

THESE TEN PEOPLE:

Tracy Graham

Stefan Poznansky

Kris Lewinski

Donna Ferarri

Sheila Trench

Pat Lee

Wesley Hall

Donald St. Martin

Victoria Schroeder

Ch'en Ling

WORDS

LOOK OVER THE FOLLOWING WORDS,

TAKING A MAXIMUM OF TWO MINUTES.

bicycle	knife
binoculars	ring
apple	cookie
sandwich	playground
doctor	fifteen
water	
hat	
shell	
library	
hands	

NUMBERS

YOU NOW HAVE FIVE MINUTES

TO LEARN THE FOLLOWING

TELEPHONE NUMBERS:

Adrian	5690234
Jon	9902378
Pauline	8209735
Andi	90234851
Mary-Anne	6523909
Judith	534782

WORD LISTS

GIVE YOURSELF FIVE MINUTES TO STUDY THESE TWO LISTS:

LIST A	LIST B
1 wine	1 clean the car
2 pepper	2 wrap presents
3 coffee	3 feed the dog
4 lettuce	4 wash the dishes
5 fish	5 paint the kitchen
6 mushrooms	6 fix the bathtub
7 pie	7 mail letters
8 ice cream cone	8 call Richard
9 potato	9 buy present for Charlie
10 leek	10 return library books

HOW WELL DID YOU DO?

NOW IS YOUR CHANCE TO TEST YOUR NEW MEMORY SKILLS.
REMEMBER TO STAY CALM AND ENJOY THE CHALLENGE.

NAMES AND FACES

HOW MANY NAMES CAN YOU RECALL FROM THE LIST?
GIVE YOURSELF ONE POINT FOR A FIRST NAME AND ONE
POINT FOR A SURNAME.

NUMBERS

HOW MANY OF THE TELEPHONE NUMBERS CAN YOU REMEMBER?
THERE ARE FIVE POINTS AVAILABLE FOR EACH NUMBER
RECALLED PERFECTLY.

Adrian ....   Andi ....

Jon ....   Mary-Anne ....

Pauline ....   Judith ....

WORD LISTS

TRY WRITING DOWN LISTS A AND B FROM MEMORY, THEN CHECK
FOR ACCURACY. GIVE YOURSELF ONE POINT FOR EACH ITEM
REMEMBERED IN THE CORRECT POSITION.

	LIST A		LIST B
1		1	
2		2	
3		3	
4		4	
5		5	
6		6	
7		7	
8		8	
9		9	
10		10	

NAMES AND FACES

TRY WRITING DOWN THE WORD LIST FROM MEMORY.
THERE WERE FIFTEEN WORDS: YOU SCORE TWO POINTS
FOR EACH ONE YOU RECALL.

FURTHER PRACTICE

AS WELL AS PRACTICING MEMORY STRATEGIES IN YOUR DAILY LIFE, YOU SHOULD RETURN TO THESE PAGES REGULARLY FOR AN EXTRA CHALLENGE.

The memory needs regular exercise, and you can use these sets of information to complete mental workouts whenever you have spare time. Practice learning these names and faces and word lists on the next page, and create challenges for yourself by memorizing longer and longer sequences of numbers and cards. Monitor your accuracy and speed, and always commit yourself to improving your performance.

NAMES

Christine McCarron	Norman Baring	Claude Diaz
Blake Fields	Harry Sale	Sarah Taylor
Arlene Danson	Debbie Singer	Philippa Carr
Philippe Rondeau	Cole Cooper	Sean Wilson
Caitlin Meredith	Rikki Donovan	Frances Hume
Dieter Langer	Bianca Burton	Jackie Banderas
Craig Blackstone	Jimmy O'Neil	Steve Parkin
Linda Welsh	Brad Scot	Bill Menendez
Donny Renaldo	Helena Dubois	Yuri Pope
Marc Crumb	Ronald Martino	Larry Harper

WORDS

cake	disaster	hollow	chicken	meander
broken	workman	mine	flower	volcano
lemon	mouse	baby	scissors	evil
hat	shoes	red	short	Wednesday
comb	shadow	zinc	bargain	wine
ruler	portable	money	pink	coast
nail	comfort	jealousy	cherry	heckle
footstep	railway	sober	goddess	dice
lightning	lace	fruit	square	leave
bishop	machine	vase	level	yes
dog	wool	balloon	cup	hoop
yellow	swallow	stand	cone	sharpening
field	soul	hungry	suitcase	ordinary
tile	apple	bandage	well	tortoise
miniature	zebra	chair	gloves	pear
button	button	jump	kitchen	hello
ship	ship	garden	pin	keep
glass	glass	over	rebel	ground
pillow	pillow	yard	cool	electricity
stall	stall	whole	mouse	eternal
	chess			
	head			
	worse			
	letters			
	ball			
	light			

NUMBERS

2 0 0 1 3 0 4 2 9 7 8 6 3 5 9 1 6 3 0 9 6 3 9 2 0 5 7 9 2 6 0 3 9 3 1 9 2 6 3 0 7 9 5 6 3 8 7 9 2 6

3 0 2 0 8 5 3 0 9 0 5 3 9 3 0 9 0 5 0 3 4 9 5 7 9 9 8 4 3 0 9 2 0 5 3 6 9 2 3 0 4 2 3 0 7 4 6 5 3 7

8 6 5 3 7 8 6 3 5 0 9 6 0 3 5 6 0 9 4 5 2 6 0 4 9 5 8 5 3 7 9 5 9 3 4 5 1 7 6 8 9 2 3 1 2 9 9 5 3 2

4 7 3 2 1 4 9 5 7 4 2 0 9 0 1 9 8 0 8 9 5 2 9 5 0 2 9 7 8 2 0 7 8 9 4 3 7 5 9 2 0 1 5 0 2 6 9 5 4 2

9 6 7 5 2 6 0 2 0 4 6 9 5 7 9 8 3 1 2 4 3 2 0 9 5 5 5 2 0 5 6 2 5 8 2 0 6 3 4 1 3 0 8 5 3 4 1 0 7 9

CARDS

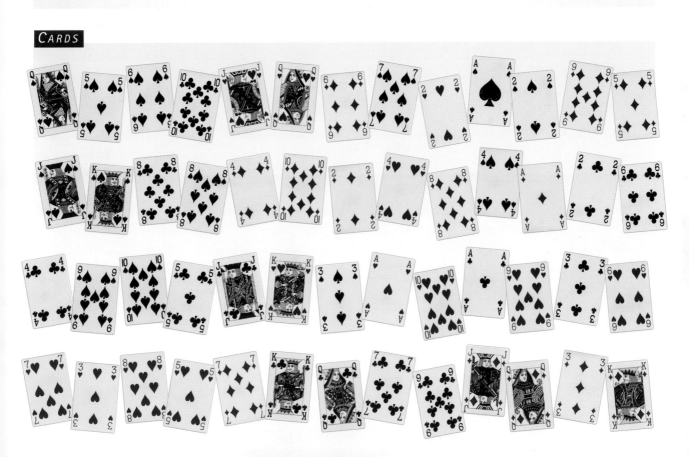

TEST YOURSELF

To make the most of your new memory skills, challenge yourself to learn information that is outside your everyday experiences. Choose unfamiliar subjects that aren't covered in this book. By exposing yourself to new types of information, you can adapt your memory techniques, strengthen your mind control, and widen your overall knowledge.

INDEX

CREDITS

QUARTO WOULD LIKE TO ACKNOWLEDGE AND THANK THE IMAGE BANK FOR PICTURES USED IN THIS BOOK: TOP LEFT PAGE 22 AND TOP LEFT PAGE 156. ALL OTHER PHOTOGRAPHS ARE THE PROPERTY OF QUARTO.

QUARTO WOULD ALSO LIKE TO THANK JONATHAN FERGUSON FOR THE LOAN OF PHOTOGRAPHIC PROPS USED THROUGHOUT THE BOOK.